YALMAMBIRRA
A Jigsaw Puzzle

MMH PRESS

Published by MMH Press 2021

Because of the dynamic nature of the Internet, any web addresses or links contained in this book may have changed since publication and may no longer be vaild. The views expressed in this work are solely those of the author and do not necessarily reflect the views of the publisher and the publisher hereby disclaims any responsibility for them.

A catalogue record for this work is available from the National Library of Australia

Yalmambirra/MMH Press

ISBN: 978-0-6450521-7-6
(paperback)

ISBN: 978-0-6450966-0-6
(ebook)

ACKNOWLEDGEMENTS

I wish to acknowledge that the recollections presented in the following pages are simply the recollections of my life and not of others. The people, places and events remembered are written from my personal viewpoint, perspectives and opinions. Having listened to family and friends over the years I have come to understand that they may have a different version of things; indeed we all have this thing called perception which is dynamic and ever shifting in nature. However, my memories (good or bad, right or wrong) are still my memories, and it is these memories that, collectively, have formed the jigsaw puzzle that is my life.

I also want to acknowledge the people who have helped by contributing photographs and assisted with the technical aspects of putting something like this together, especially Margaret (the annual Parkes photos), Kat (for being my technical assistant and for putting all the pictures into the story), and Ilona (for the creation of banner pictures, spell-checking and coffee chats).

Contents

PART TWO

CHAPTER FIVE

CHAPTER SIX

CHAPTER SEVEN

CHAPTER EIGHT

Introduction

My life began as John Henry Joseph Clegg. I was born in the year 1950 to Robert and Ida Clegg and was their fourth child to enter the world. There would be more! My mother had twelve children in total, though sadly two of my siblings were taken from Mum and Dad very soon after they were born.

The family moved around a lot and finally put down roots in a suburb of Cabramatta called Mt. Pritchard. We all grew up in this house, even though some of us had been born elsewhere. My life story begins in this house and is the starting point for everything else that followed; the experiences and people that I was fortunate, or not, to interact with, were all products of my life at 16 Grainger Avenue, Mt. Pritchard.

I write this story simply to convey my life and times in Australia, my land and my home. There are parts of the story that will not make for happy reading; but I have come to understand that this is both inevitable and unavoidable.

I have written this story in two distinct sections. Part One includes my earliest memories of people, places and events, the many jobs I had, my marriage to Denise and the birth of my sons, John, Jamie, Daniel and Jeremy. It contains my feelings on the passing of first, my father, and then my Mother into the spirit world, along with thoughts from my brothers and sisters and some of the friends that I was fortunate to have.

Part Two looks at my life after Mum and Dad. The second section looks at my change in name, my life in Albury and surrounds, my marriages to Mary-Anne and Paula, the birth of my son Jacob, my work life and the friendships I made and continue to make until I feel the jigsaw puzzle is complete.

It is my hope that, as you read my story, you will understand how my life, and events that shaped my life, are all just pieces of a jigsaw puzzle. All the people that I have met, all the things that I have done, and all the places that I have been, are simply pieces of this puzzle. When is life's jigsaw puzzle complete? And when does one know when to finish a story like this? I don't know, but maybe my story will only end when I have a more comfortable and peaceful life, and when all the pieces of the jigsaw finally come together…maybe. Having said that, I hope you enjoy my jigsaw puzzle.

PART ONE

CHAPTER ONE

My Nan and Pop

I remember my Nan and Pop. They were really very nice people and would visit us as often as they could. Sometimes we would visit them and we all had really great times with them. I do remember being allowed to run through cornfields and being allowed to put my hands in the lolly jar, but only under strict supervision! Nan and Pop most always gave us a hanky or comb as presents. We understood that they hardly had any money and we were grateful for our little gifts.

My most special memory of Nan and Pop was the last Christmas they spent with us. All the family were there. Mothers, fathers, brothers, sisters, aunts and uncles, cousins and nieces and nephews had all come to our house in St Mary's. There was also a special guest that year... Santa Claus! Nan and Pop were great teachers in their own right and would always tell a story if we asked them to—and we often did. In all the years that I knew them, I never heard them say a cross word to each other, or to others.

Pop was in World War One in the First Australian Light Horse. He represented his people and country well but was subjected to racism when he returned from the war. More information can be found in the Attachments section of this story. Nan and Pop were married for over fifty years and loved each other tremendously. Both have now passed into the spirit world where they also look out for us.

A MANSION

Early on in our lives, we lived at Toongabbie in Mum's brother's house. Mum's brother Bertie was married to Molly and we shared their house for what seemed like an eternity! For some strange reason Mum and Dad thought it would be good for us if we drank a glass of kerosene and sugar mixed together, every day. It tasted horrible but they obviously thought it would 'clean' us out and therefore be good for us!

One night, Dad asked some of us to come to the bonfire because he had some news for us. Towards the end of the night Mum and Dad pulled us aside and told us that we were going to move. We had gotten a Housing Commission house in Mt Pritchard! This ranked as one of the best days of my life.

The house in Mt. Pritchard was number 16 on Grainger Avenue. And what a house it was! It had a kitchen, dining room, lounge room, bathroom, laundry, hallway and four bedrooms. This house was a mansion! It had a big back yard and front yard where we could play and have lots of fun…and we did. The majority of my brothers and sisters were conceived at 16 Grainger Avenue.

MY MOTHER AND MY FATHER

Mum had twelve children. We do not know where the two stolen children are. Mum and Dad brought us up as best they could given the circumstances they endured in their own daily lives. Dad loved a beer. He would stop at the Cabramatta Inn on his way home from work and play cards with his mates and then come home. He got drunk a lot. And when he got drunk he would hit Mum. Mum was a strong lady, but the continual beatings eventually wore her down. I remember coming home one day and hearing Mum screaming and the kids yelling and crying. I was fifteen at the time. When I got into the lounge room, Dad was hitting Mum and the walls were covered in blood…Mum's blood.

I knew we couldn't go on living like this and I always thought that one day he would kill her. One day I grabbed Dad, pulling him away from Mum. The kids got her and took her out of the house. It was just me and Dad now. I told him that I couldn't let him hit Mum anymore and so we went into the hallway, closed all the doors and fought each other. When it was over, Dad had a serious eye injury and he was bleeding badly. I drove him to hospital and waited for him so I could drive him home. I didn't even have a license back then. We drove in silence for a while when Dad finally said: "Why didn't you do this a long time ago?" Well, how could I, when Dad used to earn money boxing?

We drove around for a while and had a talk about lots of things and then I drove him home. Mum was waiting for him and she was worried about him. This was the night that Dad finally stopped hitting Mum; it was also the night he gave up drinking. This night would forever change Mum and Dad's relationship, and mine and Dad's relationship, too. Dad became not just my father, but my best friend and life would again become great in the Clegg household.

I loved going to work with Dad on Sundays. I had to run the three miles to the train station because Dad had really big strides, but it was always worth it because I loved the steam trains that took us to work and back home again.

After Dad stopped drinking, he and Mum moved to Perth, but they only stayed for a little while. When they came back, they moved again, this time to Warwick Farm; but again, before too long they moved. This time it was to Parkes, where they remained until they both passed away.

As a boy growing up in a violent environment, I quickly learned not to cry. I had to be strong in all that I did. If I cried, then I would get another belting, so I decided not to cry anymore, and these feelings have stayed with me all the days of my life. With all the many family members I have buried, from Nan and Pop, to Uncles and Aunts, I have never cried. I didn't even cry when Dad passed into the spirit world. Nor did I cry when Mum finally took her place beside Dad. This is not something I am proud of, but I have become hardened to shedding tears.

Mum was a Wiradjuri lady and was the real force behind the family. She was a very hardworking lady and raised us as best she could with what she had. With ten kids to look after Mum had to do it the hard way, but as we got older, we helped out as best we could. Mum always tried to provide good meals for us, tried her best to make sure we went to school and got an education and was always there for us when things went wrong. I have always regarded my Mother as the best and strongest lady that I have ever met.

I remember one day when Mum was arguing with Dad and she had chased him out the front door, into the front yard and down the street. Mum had a kitchen fork in her hand and she threw the fork at Dad. It stuck him in the back and he began yelling, "she's killed me, she's killed me!" If I remember correctly, I just laughed and laughed! Then, after things settled down Mum took Dad back inside to check out what damage had been done.

Mum played the violin. Sometimes she would play solo and sometimes she would play with Jimmy Little, and sometimes she would play when her sister sang. When Mum played the violin, I would get tears in my eyes…she was fantastic! Mum's sister Lorna was a soprano and one of the first to test the acoustics in The Sydney Opera House. I remember one day when The Ngan Girra Festival was on at an area known as Mungabareena Reserve in Albury. Every year this festival was held where various people were invited to attend and, of course, perform.

This one year Jimmy Little was going to perform. I didn't tell Mum or Lorna that he was going to be there. They had both performed with Jimmy over the years but hadn't seen him in over thirty odd years. I told Jimmy that Mum and Lorna were in the audience and asked him if would he like to catch up. So there was Jimmy singing, and there was Mum and Lorna sitting in the audience with tears in their eyes. When Jimmy had finished singing, I brought him over to where Mum and Lorna were sitting. Then all three were crying, and big hugs and kisses were the order of the day. It was such a great moment in their lives and, of course, in mine. There are some articles on Lorna and Jimmy in the attached section at the end of this book.

Lorna and me at the Ngan Girra Festival just before meeting Jimmy.

My Mother was what some would call a 'one in a million.' Mum was my earliest role model and raised me with good values and attitudes. If this had not been the case, then I am sure I would have been someone very different.

Dad was always a good provider. He hardly missed a day at work and he worked very, very hard for his family. Sometimes however, bills would arrive at the same time when money was scarce. My father may have been a man of many contradictions, but he had a great sense of survival. When the electricity would get cut off for not paying the bill, Dad would bypass the meter-box and start it up again!

In an attempt to save money and still provide enjoyment for his family, Dad hired a TV. Not any TV mind you; but a slot TV. We put two bob (twenty cents) in the slot behind the TV and we could watch it for one hour. Half-way through a movie the money would run out and we wouldn't have enough to put any more back in…this began a back and forth dance to the neighbour's place for change or a loan!

We kids also knew a little about survival. When we wanted to watch TV we would get some sticky tape and tape it to the coin and put it in the slot. When the time ran out we simply pulled it out and put the same coin back in! We used to get into all sorts of trouble when the rental man came for his money, only to find there was one coin—or none at all—in the box.

One day, Dad decided to get some pigeons and I think that he raced some of them. I do remember that we ate pigeon pie sometimes! And of course there were dogs. I'm not sure how many dogs lived at 16 Grainger Ave, but it was a lot. Most died after getting dog disease, with most being buried in the backyard. Guess you could say that our backyard was a pet cemetery of sorts.

Whilst Dad was a good provider, he was also a bit of a kleptomaniac. He was always looking out for opportunities that would provide additional family support. I'm not sure how it happened or when, but I was, for a while, his 'getaway driver.' One very early morning, Dad woke me up and said, "Let's go for a drive." This, I soon learned, was Dad's way of saying 'let's go steal something.' To be perfectly honest, I know Dad only did this to support his family; he never did it for self-gain.

So here we were on this dark, lonely street, and Dad told me to stay in the car and sound the horn if anything happened to me. The only thing that happened was I fell asleep! The next thing I knew, Dad was trying to wake me, saying, "Hurry, help me put these in the boot and let's get out of here." I got out of the car to open the boot and there were twenty sets of golf clubs lined up against the fence. Dad had raided the local golf club! When I saw Dad later that afternoon, I asked him what he had done with them. He told me that he had taken all of them to the local 'hock shop' and got rid of them all. What hock shop takes twenty sets of golf clubs without asking where they came from? That one is still a mystery to me.

There was also the time when Mum asked me into the bedroom. She was lying in bed and told me to close the door. When I did so, she lifted the sheet up and there was all this money. Hundreds and hundreds of dollar notes! Mum explained that Dad wanted me to take some of the money and go to the races in an effort to 'launder' it. I went to the races and lost nearly all of what Mum had given me, which was around $100...a lot of money in those days!

With such a large family to feed, both Mum and Dad would despair if there wasn't enough food to go around, so one day Dad asked me to go with him to steal some chickens. Trouble was, chickens were not very quiet things when you tried to catch them. They made enough noise to wake people up and then we had to get away fast; thankfully, Dad had put some dead ones in a safe place and when all the noise had died down, we went back and collected them. We had some funny stories around the dinner table that night.

Dad got a little sick down the track. He had some pills he had to take for his heart and one day when he and some of his sons went fishing, Mum had packed his heart tablets. We spread out along the banks of the river and started fishing; Dad decided he would move upstream a little. Even though he was out of sight, we thought he would be ok. As time passed we decided to catch up with him, and just as we did, he fell head first into the river! We thought he had had a heart attack.

When we pulled him out he said he didn't know what happened to him. We went home and only then did we find out what really happened; Mum stood there fuming because she thought he was drunk. Upon discovering that he was, in fact, sober, she then asked Dad if he had taken his tablets. Mum checked the bag for the remaining tablets and found that she had put the sleeping pills in his bag instead of the heart tablets! Dad had simply gone to sleep!

Both Mum and Dad played golf. Mum won a few club championships, too. She would grip the club with two hands, and when she made the backswing she'd let the club go and catch it again and then hit the ball! Dad played golf left-handed even though he was right-handed. He also won a few championships. I loved being Dad's caddy, but I don't think I ever caddied for Mum.

Dad played Rugby League for Mt. Pritchard (Mounties) at Cook Park. He was an ok player and we used to go watch him play. Dad decided to become a referee after a while and he was ok at that, too. At one game Mum and some of the kids were watching the game when Dad had made a decision that Mum wasn't happy about. She grabbed her umbrella and ran on to the field and started hitting Dad on the head with it! Mum also played Rugby League for a ladies' side and she was a force to be reckoned with, but after a few seasons she decided that it was time to retire and she gave it up.

Dad liked going rabbit hunting. It helped put food on the table too. I went with him a few times and one time when we had ferrets some funny things happened. We would find the rabbit warrens and Dad would put the nets over the holes and then put the ferret down one of them. Sometimes the ferret would behave and sometimes it would stay in the hole eating the baby rabbits and then go to sleep!

Dad had taken to bringing a garden mattock with him so he could dig the ferret out. One time Dad didn't see the ferret come out after the rabbits and, cursing, he grabbed the mattock and started digging. After a while I noticed something moving in the grass. A closer look revealed that the ferret had indeed come out of the rabbit hole and was sitting in the shade, watching Dad digging up the warren. I can't remember what happened to the ferret but I don't think Dad gave it a hug!

THE PASSING OF MY FATHER

Mum and Dad found a nice little house in Parkes and we spent some good times there until Dad got very sick. I had always thought of my father as being indestructible, but this didn't turn out to be true. When Dad got sick, he was in and out of hospital more times than the people that worked there!

I always tried to get to Parkes to visit Mum and Dad as often as I could. Whenever I visited Mum would make some good food and I would sit and chat with Dad over a beer. Dad had taken to having one or two beers, but only when we visited…he just wanted to be one of the boys again. Dad smoked a lot and this I think caused his illness; eventually his hospital visits became longer and longer and more frequent and we all knew something was wrong.

Mum called me one day to tell me that Dad had gone into hospital again and I told her I was going to drive up to see him the next day. I was on the golf course with my friend Jon and my brother Darryl, when Denise drove into the golf course sounding the horn of the car…I knew something was wrong. Denise announced that Dad had passed away in hospital. It was the tenth day of June. The thing is that I always had this feeling that Dad would choose a time to go when it would affect someone in a kind of funny way. So he waited until we were on the golf course and just four days shy of my birthday!

Darryl and I drove up to Parkes to help with things and to give Mum some support. Dad was still in the hospital and we were allowed to go in and see him and say goodbye, and my sister Deb had some roses for each of us to place on Dad's chest. I placed the rose on Dad and I kissed him, and then I went outside. The others followed. Mum stayed in the room because she said she wanted to say something to Dad in private and she wanted some time alone with her husband of so many years. I never asked Mum what she said to Dad…it was her and Dad's business, not mine. Up to this point, this had been the saddest moment in my life.

Steve, Pete, Darryl, Geoff and Rob carrying Dad. I was also there but not in the photo.

We had two funerals for Dad. The first was held in Parkes and the second was held in Orange. A lot of people were coming from Sydney and so it we decided to have a service in Orange to avoid people having to travel further. Dad was cremated and his ashes were scattered on the Parkes golf course where Rob had put them, because Dad played lots of golf there with family and his friends. The photo below is one of family and friends at the annual golf day.

As the oldest male in the family, it was my task to deliver my father's eulogy. What I remember most was looking out into a sea of faces of family and friends and seeing the sadness that lay there; and there, in the second row was my son Jeremy, crying his eyes out. That made it even sadder for me. When we had all returned to our own homes I took Jeremy aside on the front steps of our house; he was still very, very sad, so I thought I would try to explain some things to him to help him in his hurting. I pointed to a big star in the sky and told him that the star was my father, his Poppy, and that Poppy would always be in the sky, looking over us and out for us, every single day.

I miss my father very much. It seems to me that a very, very vital piece of the jigsaw puzzle has gone missing, but the reality is that it hasn't really, because he is always with us. Dad was a man used to getting his own way, but he turned his life around so he could spend the rest of his life with the lady he loved most of all. Dad knew what he had done was wrong, and he was willing to change everything—and he did all of that because he loved his wife very, very much. Mum had forgiven him and had given him a second chance. I speak with Dad every day now; although I don't remember ever telling Dad that I loved him, either as a young boy or in my adult life. This has caused me to question a lot of things about myself. Dad is now my guardian angel. My father is still that star in the sky and he looks over us and looks out for us, and all I have to do is talk to him and let him know what I need and how he can help me. Dad can't fix everything of course, but I know that if he can help me, he always will…I simply need to talk to him.

THE PASSING OF MY MOTHER

Mum lived in the house that she had shared with Dad for a little while, but after a while she moved into a small unit. Then she moved from there into a small house. Darryl would fix up the garden for her and do all the mowing and stuff so the place always looked nice for her. But even though Mum was a very strong lady, there was a time when she started to get a little sick. Her illness got to the stage where the family were worried that she couldn't look after herself, so it was suggested that we move Mum into a nursing home. Mum picked out the place she wanted to go to and she stayed there.

The family used to visit her and she would tell stories, and most of them would revolve around her and Dad. But sometimes she would speak of her sister Lorna. Lorna and Mum used to be in a band of sorts with Jimmy Little, with Mum playing the violin and Lorna singing. Information on Lorna and Jimmy can be found in the Attachments section at the end of the story. Mum got sicker after that and was eventually diagnosed with Alzheimer's disease. Her memory slowly deteriorated and she found it hard to remember things the way she used to; then it got to the point where Mum couldn't remember who we were. I used to visit her, but it was hard to see my Mother like that and it hurt a lot and so I preferred to remember Mum as she was—and not as a very, very ill lady.

I remember when I received the phone call from Rob telling me that Mum passed away. My Mother passed away on August 27, 2015, and that day a new, bright star was born in the sky above us, right next to Dad. The funeral for Mum was held in Forbes and there were a lot of people and all the family there to say goodbye to her. Mum was buried in Forbes where she was born, laid to rest next to her Mum and Dad.

Mum's grave site.

Mum is now with her husband of so many years and I believe they are very, very happy together in the spirit world. I will always remember my Mother, and since she has gone, I speak to her every day, just as I do Dad. I miss her very, very much.

Before Mum got really ill, she told me about her stolen children; they were taken from her when they were born. Mum told me that the Doctors had told her that the first one had died because it was born with no skin. The second one, the Doctors said, was stillborn. But Mum knew otherwise; she knew that both children were normal and had been taken away from her. Mum was a Wiradjuri lady and she only told me this after Dad had died. Mum revealed that Dad had been a stolen child too, and that she never knew where his real family came from. Mum and Dad had kept the fact that we were Indigenous a secret because they didn't want to lose their children. They had kept this secret for all those years because they were afraid that the welfare would come and take the rest of their children. When Dad died I tried to get his 'white' brother to tell me about him, but sadly there was just this huge wall of silence—and so, to this day, we do not know anything about Dad or his real family.

CHAPTER TWO

Memories

I wasn't always a good son. I did some things that broke Mum's heart and made her cry. I recall one day that, for a dare, I set fire to the local community hall. Mum was devastated, because my punishment was that I was to spend the next eleven months in a boy's home in Mittagong, away from family and friends. As an eleven year old boy, I thought this was one of the worst things that ever happened to me. It did, however, open my eyes and from then on I tried to be a much better son…it was a good lesson to learn.

I got really sick in the boy's home after contracting rheumatic fever and I had to spend three months in the hospital under daily care. When one contracts rheumatic fever it limits what one can do physically, because it is believed to weaken the heart. Since there wasn't much I could do besides eat, they force-fed me vegetables most days, though I didn't like vegetables much. What they didn't know was that there was a knot/hole under the bed, and when they left me alone with the meal I would put all my vegetables in the hole…there must have been really big rats under that place! Many, many times I was forced to stand on cold concrete if I even looked at someone the wrong way. I tried to escape from the home three times but they always caught me and brought me back, which only resulted in more canes across the back of the hands and more vegetables. It was such a great day when, at nearly twelve years of age they finally said I could go home.

I didn't like school at all and would use every trick in the book to get out of going. I would play truant as often as I could, and so, by the age of twelve I started working with Dad instead. I remember sweeping floors in the pipe factory and I thought it was the best thing since sliced bread! I got to work with Dad every day and get paid for it and knew I couldn't ask for much better than that. When I wasn't working at the pipe factory, I had a job on the milk-run, because I wanted to save up for a bike. I had to start work at around 3am in the morning no matter the weather, winter or summer. Mum would always wake me up and serve me toast or a hot bowl of porridge and a hot cup of tea to get me on my way.

I saved the money for the bike; trouble was, I didn't have it for very long before I broke it! My brothers and I used to time each other to see who was the fastest around the block. Coming around the corner at Grainger Avenue at full steam I failed to see the taxi coming the other way. Many days later one of my shoes was found on top of the telegraph pole! All I got were a few stitches on my right hand, which was ok for someone who had gone through the front windscreen and out the driver's side window of the car. It would have helped to know there were no brakes on the bike!

We also used to race each other around the block pushing car tyres, and of course there were the billy-carts too. When we got tired of racing each other we decided to take the billy-carts to an area that we called the 'grassy hill.' Now, this hill was fairly steep and had lots of grass on it, hence its name and our goal was to race each other down it and try to not have a spill or wipeout on the gravel road waiting for us at the bottom. There were many times when we would take lots of skin off our legs because we fell out or tipped over on the gravel road, so it was decided to get a garbage bin and put it at the bottom, hoping that would stop us. I'm not sure how many billy-carts had brakes but my one didn't!

My brothers and I and joined with the other fellas in Grainger Ave and we played football and cricket in the street. We would tackle each other in the middle of the road on the hard bitumen, and when we played cricket, we would put the stumps in the centre of the road. Grainger Ave was a fairly busy road and when cars came down the road, someone would call out "car coming" and we would have to stop play and wait until the car passed before we could start up again. It really took a long time just to play one game of footy and cricket!

In the park on Grainger Ave there was a see-saw and some swings. I spent a lot of time on the swings. One day the brothers and some friends decided to make the ground under and around the swings a lot softer so we didn't get hurt if we fell off. Well, not being content with just swinging, as well as being the daredevils that we were, we decided to see how far someone could travel through the air after jumping off the swing. One would get the swing going really fast and then take a giant leap of faith, letting go at just the right moment. Then we would measure how far each jumper had travelled to see who the winner was. Looking back, I'm not sure how we didn't break any bones!

As I got older I needed a car. Dad went guarantor for me and I got a second-hand, two-tone green FB Holden. It broke down a lot of the time so I had to get another one, and this one was a second-hand FC Holden that I painted inside black and orange because I was a Tiger's football supporter. I had many more cars after that and in every single one of them I had a smash. In one of the accidents I had, it was raining very hard and the road was very slippery when I came around the corner, sliding into the gutter. I kept going, careening across the road to the other side, through a fence, running down some trees until I came to rest in someone's front yard. All of this happened with a car load of girls! I got them out and we quickly ran off. Dad was not very happy with me that day, and Mum was really worried about what the police would say or do, but they never came.

Dad gave me his car one day. He'd had it for a long time but couldn't drive it anymore. I had to go to Parkes to pick it up, but on the way back it broke down and so I sold it to one of my uncles.

I was always good friends with the boys next door and sometimes we would get into a little strife; sometimes on our own, sometimes with a little help. Two incidents of that time really stand out in my mind. The first time was when we were at the local shops; some words were exchanged and a fight broke out with lots of promises of revenge. I'm pretty sure that Darryl started everything over a girl. As we were walking back home, we had just reached the top of Grainger Avenue when a car full of guys pulled up next to us. They wound down their window and a voice inside asked, "Ok, who started the fight at the shops?" We all said "not us" and then someone from inside the car yelled, "Right, get the guns out!" We all ran zigzag, all the way down Grainger Avenue to the sounds of bullets whizzing around our ears! It was a very interesting moment, to say the least.

The second time, was when I was playing cards next door. There came a knock on the door and naturally I got up to see who it was. I looked outside and then closed the door. I told everyone to look outside. There were around fifty or sixty blokes with baseball bats and other stuff wanting to fight us. Us. Six blokes playing cards. I remember asking one of them to hop over the fence so we could sort things out peacefully. I was just about to resolve everything with the army of men just outside the door, when the owner of the house we were playing cards in said, "stuff all this talking!" and took a swing, hitting the bloke I was talking with. Well, then it was on, all up and down the street, back and forth for what seemed like ages.

Dad heard all the noise from his lounge chair and stuck his head out the window, yelling, "Stop all the noise or I'll call the cops!" Even in the midst of the fighting I can still remember having a little chuckle, because Dad was a well known fighter and all he had to do to end it was to come out and give us a hand. The fight ended when Darryl hit one of the guys on the right side of his head and I clopped the same guy on the left side at the same time. He went down in the gutter and didn't move. They picked him up and left grumbling something about coming back with more blokes, but that was the end of it.

I didn't have my first beer until I was nineteen years of age. I was working at the hat factory at the time and everyone used to have a beer at the pub at lunchtime. I used to go with them, but I'd never have a beer. This time though, I did. I have been drunk a few times, but I have never let beer or anything else detract from what I had to do. I have never hit anyone because I was drunk…a lesson I'd already learnt! I had my first shave when I was just twelve years old. Dad was talking to a neighbour and Mum had wanted him to come in and shave because they were going out. I remember asking Dad if I could have a shave for him. He didn't think I was fair dinkum, but when he said ok, I went and had my first shave!

I also played league for Mounties. At every home game at half time the players would get one or two cans of beer to drink while the coach gave us a pep talk. I was hopeless at running with football boots on and so I decided to play barefoot. At one game I was playing on the wing and it was my job to mark the opposing winger. Trouble was, he was the NSW beach sprint champion! I got a bit of a write-up in the local paper following that game after getting beat 105 to 0.

WORK I DID

I actually worked with Dad twice. The first time was sweeping floors at the pipe factory; but I soon got promoted to driving the tractor that pulled the clay pipes out into the holding yard. One day I forgot to put the brake on and the tractor took off and hit a stack of pipes, breaking 600 pipes! The boss, who was Dad's 'white brother' said I had two choices: either I had to leave or get the sack. So I left. Not long after I got my job back, but this time I was working with Dad and our job was to cook the pipes in big ovens. It was great, especially when we did the night shift and there was only me and Dad there.

I have worked in lots of places and had different jobs because I really didn't know quite what it was that I wanted to do with my life. I have worked as a brickie's labourer, a builder's labourer, a painter, a concreter, concreter's labourer; I've worked as a machinist, in cotton chipping, made silo bases, made Akubra hats, worked in a rope factory put handles on skipping ropes, worked on the railway, tried my hand at landscaping and greyhound racing, have even worked in a pub. I've made pre-fabricated garages, concrete baths, sinks and steps, made stock feed, worked on cars, worked as a cleaner and postman, worked on a milk-run, picked up sticks in a paddock, worked on councils and water-boards, and have even worked in an ice-cream van.

I also put fridge magnets on real estate stickers, tried fork-lifting and tractor driving, dabbled as a furniture removalist, worked in a signal box on the railway and put razor wire up in jails with Darryl. I've made biscuits at Arnott's and crumpets for Buttercup Bakeries, worked in a flour mill, done fencing, sold dog food, run Indigenous cultural talks with my brother Rob, performed archaeological surveys and served time in the army. I worked as a cook in Kentucky Fried Chicken, been a bartender in a wine bar, trimmed trees with Darryl, and today have just recently retired from my position as a lecturer and Koori Academic (Wiradjuri) with Charles Sturt University.

But when I look back at it all, I realise that all my life has been like this. I was just never sure that I was in the right place, doing the right thing at the right time. Many of the jobs had certain elements to them that were learning experiences, but more often than not they trigger some not-so-fond, memories.

Rob and I thought at one time we'd like to start our own business. We reckoned that hiring out golf carts would bring in some good money, and we knew that if we put a good plan together, then the bank would lend us the money to start us off. So we approached a number of golf courses and asked if we could set up business; but only one agreed. We shopped around for the best deals on carts and were nearly ready to set everything up when it started raining! It rained for days and days and days, and that closed the golf course down for weeks. In the end we decided that it was too risky to go ahead with it—we would have gone broke in the first few weeks, so reluctantly we pulled the pin.

Cotton chipping in Wee Waa was a real eye opener for me and was a strange experience, because I actually paid to get the job through an employment agency. I was the only black fella on a bus of around fifty men and we had to stay in the contractor's compound, which was some miles from where we were doing the actual work. The compound had buildings designated for sleeping in, with each room having eight beds. No one wanted to share a room with a black fella though, so I had the whole room to myself, which I didn't mind at all. We had to get up at 3.30 am every morning, have breakfast, get changed into work gear, grab a hoe, and then hop onto a truck with fifty other blokes where we would stand like sardines for a good eighty kilometres. The cotton fields were about 500 meters wide and about a kilometre long, our job, to chip out all the weeds! Boy, that was real hard work. When I wanted a drink of water, I had to call out for the water boy and about half an hour later he would finally show up. Lunchtime was a real shambles, too. I would hear the lunch bell go, and if I was way down the other end of the row, by the time I actually got my lunch, it would be time to get back to work. I pretty much ate on the run every day that I worked there.

Now, working at Wee Waa was in a time when there were still

segregated places; there'd be one place for people like me, then there'd be a different place for the white guys. One night when I was paid (always by cheque), I had to go into town to cash it, but as always, again there were two lines of people: one for the white guys and one for the black fellas. The white line was always first to get their cheques cashed…funny how the shop always ran out of money when I was getting close to the head of the line!

One night there was a big fight in town; people from the white pub and people from the black pub started throwing cans of beer at each other. I found a bag and started collecting all the full cans, so I never paid for any beer while I was in Wee Waa. The problem with the job was that we were told that we could work from sunrise to sunset, seven days a week—but that wasn't the truth, because we were not allowed to work weekends. I stayed for around three weeks and then decided to hitch-hike home, because by then I'd had enough.

Stick-picking I remember was a great job! All you had to do was stand on the side of the trailer behind a tractor and bend down and pick up the sticks in the paddocks. Trouble was that the tractor didn't stop. There were plenty of times when I would grab at what I thought was a stick, only to find that it was a tree root and I would get pulled off the tractor and end up lying in the deep, red dust of the paddock! Then I would have to run and catch up with the tractor and throw my body back on it to keep working.

Sometimes my brother Pete and I would take it in turns driving the tractor. There was however one time, and let me emphasis that it was only *one* time, that we let Rob drive the tractor…because it was a big, big mistake! You have to imagine what the conditions were like; it was dry, as in drought dry, heaps and heaps of red dust and of course, real hot and gusty winds. The problem was that Rob would drive straight into the wind, causing red dust to go flying out from under the tractor wheels and directly on to us! We were certainly a sight, that's for sure, but we wouldn't let him drive again…we reckon that the mad bugger did it deliberately!

One of the most eventful times in my working life was at a place called Lake Cargellico in New South Wales. It was roughly five hundred kilometres west of Sydney, and it was here that I worked with my brothers Pete and Darryl. It was Darryl's and my job to lay concrete bases for grain silos; after the concrete had dried it was then Pete's job to erect the silos, so we were all working in the same place, just at different times. One day after we finished work it was really hot, so we thought we'd like to go for a swim in the lake and have a few beers to cool down. Pete went home to get some gear and I sat waiting in the pub for him with a few beers. When he hadn't arrived, I decided that he must already be at the lake, and so I left the pub.

I started walking to the lake and I was only about fifty metres from the pub when I saw the police sitting there in their cruiser. They called me over to the car, and so obediently I went. The cop in the front passenger seat wound down his window and started to ask me questions; this went on for several minutes, and after answering the same questions over and over, I asked why he wanted to know. The cop in the front passenger seat suddenly opened the door, got out and grabbed me by the throat, then opened the back door and threw me in the back seat. Then he got in beside me, closed the door and started bashing me. One thing that I learned from this was that when a cop is bashing you, never hit back, so I just took what was happening, though I had no idea why.

When he finished bashing me, they drove me to the police station and took me inside. The first officer wanted to check to see if I had any warrants, when the cop who had bashed me in the car, started to bash me again. They locked me up without any explanation, and then the next morning, again without any explanation, they let me go. When I was a safe enough distance walking away from the station, I told them that I would sue them for assault, and then they told me to get out of town in a hurry. As I walked out the front gate I recognised one of the guys I had been working with and called out to him, but he just kept walking away from me faster and faster. I found out later that the reason he didn't stop was because he didn't recognise me through all the blood that was on my face.

I went to a friend's house but he wasn't home. Then I went to Pete's house and I told him what had happened and I swore that I would get back at the cop who bashed me up. We went to the home of my boss for a BBQ later that day, and he asked me and Pete if we would go across the road to get some beer and we agreed to go. When we got to the pub, who was sitting there but the cop who had bashed me the night before. He was at the bar with some guys, so I pointed at him and told Pete that this was the cop who had bashed me up, but of course he denied it.

Later that night, two cop cars pulled up at the front of Pete's house. The Sergeant came in and the cop that had bashed me kept his distance and stayed by the front door. I didn't know what to think, except that it looked like another bashing was about to happen. The Sergeant told Pete that they wanted to take me down to the cop shop and charge me with assaulting a police officer in the line of duty and for offensive behaviour in a hotel. Pete looked at me and I just looked at him…there was no need for words because right then we both knew what I was going to do next.

When the cop opened the front door of the house, I ran. I only had a shirt and shorts on, no shoes. The bindies or cat's eyes are really big in the grasses there and they were very, very sharp. I ran for a long time through the prickly grasses and they tore my feet to shreds. I came to a paddock and there were a big pile of bricks in the middle of it and so thought I could hide in the middle of them. The cops came, and then they started to use the searchlights, swinging the blinding light all over the paddock just looking for me. I thought it was a little dicey sitting there and I felt like a sitting duck; it would be only a matter of time before they found me. So when the lights were pointed in another direction I got up the nerve and quickly made a move for it. I darted to a tree and thought I would climb it and hide there. I was just about to do that but in my haste to hide from the cops I hadn't noticed that the tree was only about three meters high! It was useless to hide there, so I hid down low in the grasses and waited it out.

I eventually found my way back to Parkes and to Mum and Dad's house, and all I wanted to do was head back to Sydney. I rang the Legal Service hotline and told them what had happened. Unbeknownst to me, they then called the police, and it turned out that I had to turn myself in because now there were two more charges against me; one for assault and two counts of resisting arrest. I couldn't believe it, but then this was 1983, and things were pretty backward, and I felt as though I didn't have a leg to stand on. For the next five years the police took me to Court all over NSW, including Broken Hill, which was when my brother Steve finally went with me.

We went by train to Broken Hill and during the trip we ate nearly all of our food and drank all of the beer, leaving us with just a bottle of Coke and a tomato. We decided to walk out of town a little ways to put up our tent; in the end we found a paddock that looked to be ok about three kilometres down the road, so up went the tent and we put our heads down, ready for a good sleep. We were nearly asleep, when a lightning storm erupted overhead; being afraid of lightning myself, I nervously suggested that we head back into town but Steve didn't want to, so I told him that if lightning hit the tent poles then the tent would melt all over us. He moved really quickly then! After the storm had passed, we went back to our camp spot, but all night long all I could see were car and truck headlights coming through the tent. When we got up the next morning we could see why: we had set the tent up just metres from the side of the main road, right on a hair-pin bend!

The Court always found me guilty because I was a black fella, but after going to Court so many times I became used to it. But one time the Court found me not guilty. It was 1988 and in that year my lawyer and I decided that we would sue the police. By 1991, eight years after it had all started, we found ourselves in Bathurst Court because by then, if one wanted to take civil action against the police, it had to be in front of a jury.

The hearing lasted five days and every morning of those five days the police lawyers would offer me money: $10,000 to be exact. Every morning they offered, and every morning I would tell them where to shove it. On day five, my lawyer said that perhaps we should take the money, as he had a feeling that things were going to turn bad for us. I thought long and hard about it and finally agreed; he was right, and I just couldn't see the point in going on anymore, so I said ok. Just as my lawyer was going over to inform them, I called him back and told him to go over and tell them to shove their money. It wasn't about money. It was only ever about justice for a black fella. At the end of the day, the jury came back in with their verdict; they had found the cop guilty of assault and I was awarded $6,000 in damages. They didn't find him guilty of any of the other stuff though, and in the end he was given a promotion and moved to Parkes, ironically just up the road from Mum and Dad. Through all of this, Dad was always there for me and I knew he felt the same levels of frustration and anger as I did. Friends stick together, don't they? That is the sad story of what happened to me.

One year after Rob had moved to Townsville, he told me that I should come up and see him because the lifestyle was great and there was plenty of work and good money. I was married to my first wife Denise at the time and our baby John was only about twelve months old. I borrowed a car from Denise's father, and on the way to Townsville, the car broke down. Anyhow, the place we found ourselves in had some petrol pumps in the front yard of one of the houses. The guy who ran the pumps helped to fix the car; all he wanted for payment was the radio. I handed him the radio and we set forth again for Townsville. About fifty kilometres down the road the car broke down again. We sat by the side of the road not knowing what to do, when a guy in a ute drove up and offered to pay us for the car. He only had fifteen dollars on him; we looked at each other and shrugged. Fifteen dollars was better than nothing and so that's what we sold it for. Then we had to hitch-hike the next four hundred kilometres to Townsville.

After walking and pushing the pram with John in it for miles and miles, as well as carrying everything we had, a guy pulled over and gave us a lift. He drove us a hundred kilometres to where he and his father worked. We had nice hot showers and a hot meal and then they drove us another hundred kilometres to a halfway place, fixing it so we could get a lift into Townsville the next day. The lady who ran the halfway place let us sleep in a room for nothing and we were so grateful. The truck driver we met the next morning was willing to drive us the final two hundred kilometres into Townsville.

We had made it. We arrived in Townsville with only fifteen dollars total in our pocket. When we finally located Rob we found out that he hadn't worked for ages, there were no jobs and certainly no money to be had! We were there for a while and one day we saw an ad for two labourers on a building site, so Rob and I went down there. We spoke to a Chinese fella and he said he wanted us to dig out some trenches that had been filled in. He said he would pay us thirty dollars for the day so we went to work and we worked really hard in the stifling heat, under a scorching hot Queensland sun.

At the end of the day I went to get our pay and the fella handed me two cheques worth fifteen dollars each. He had only ever meant to pay us that much each, not the thirty dollars each we were owed. We cashed the cheques and used them to buy $15 worth of food and $15 worth of beer to drown our sorrows. At some point in the night, I decided that for trying to rip us off we should go back and fill in the trenches; so that's what we did. It took nearly eight hours to clean the trenches out but only two hours to fill them back in again! We walked away laughing, wishing we could have seen the look on the Chinese guy's face the next day. I still smile over that one.

It was in Townsville where I landed a job as a cook working in Kentucky Fried Chicken. I saved all the money that I could so that we had enough to get back home; after a few months we finally had our bus tickets out of there, and we said goodbye to Townsville, so glad to get on the bus and even happier at the thought of going home. Through it all, not once did I ever hear Denise complain about anything.

The job in the wine bar wasn't that good. I really only collected glasses sometimes, but Rob worked there too as the doorman for a while. The door was where all the trouble started, however. One night when I wasn't working, Rob was working the door and he had a friend of the family there with him who had only just started working there that night too. During the night, Rob had to stop some guys from coming in because they were troublemakers and had been told to stay away. They went away and Rob asked his friend to look after the door so he could have a break. That's when the troublemakers came back. Rob was coming back off his break just when he saw the door open; he knew what was about to happen, but he was too late. His friend was dead before he hit the ground and Rob got stabbed in the stomach. In the end, the wine bar was demolished by a Molotov cocktail. Must have been thrown by someone with a grudge, eh?

I decided to register as a greyhound owner/trainer when I was given a new greyhound. Darryl and I called the dog Magna Seven. When I was working, Darryl would exercise the dog, and when Darryl couldn't do it, then Steve would take his turn; but Steve's idea of exercising a dog was to take the bus. The dog ran very fast but in its first official race it ran last under extenuating circumstances. When they jumped out of the gates, the dog jumped last, then it started to move through on the rails. It ran too close, then it clipped the inside rail, flew through the air and hit the outside rail on the full. That was the end of Magna Seven.

I did my Army training in Wagga Wagga and it was great because I got really fit from all the daily gruesome workouts they put us through.

When I enlisted I was asked what I wanted to be. I decided that I wanted to do anything that would let me stay based close to home. About one week out from graduating we were told where we would be going. It turned out that they were going to send me to some other base in Melbourne! As soon as they told me, I decided to go AWOL.

One night I got dressed and when it was really quiet, I took off over the paddock. I had little idea of where I was going; all I knew was that I had to get away from the Base. I had called Denise earlier that week and told her what I was planning to do; she agreed and said that she would meet me on the main road going into Wagga. I ran across the paddocks and got as close as I could to the road so I could see if the Army were out looking for me…and they were.

Every time I saw a car I hid behind some bushes so no one could see me. It was really dark which helped a lot. I kept going, but eventually I needed to stop for a rest. As I was resting there in the darkness, I heard something come up behind me; I turned very slowly to see what it was and found myself looking straight into the eyes of a very, very large cow. Needless to say, I bolted! I ran through the paddocks at lightning speed, running into fences that cut my legs, but nothing would stop me and I just kept running until eventually I ran straight into a swamp! Finally, I made it to the main road, and there was Denise, waiting for me. When we got home, I became paranoid for a while that the Army might come looking for me and so I hid under the house…but they never did come. They discharged me instead.

Working in the flour mill in Parramatta was really good. Every day seemed to be different; even more so on the night shifts. At one stage it was my job to stack the bags of flour when they came off the machine. Each bag weighed between 50 and 60 kilos and I could stack around 500 to 600 bags a day. I was very fit back then and would have kept working at this job except that the flour section got sold off, so then I got moved into the pet food section. Now it was part of my job to empty the grain trucks. One day a driver asked to be unloaded and I told him that he had to go to our 'holding' site. He was a little angry about that and pulled a gun on me and demanded to be unloaded! So I did! I learned that you never argue when you're looking down the barrel of a gun!

Sometimes the grain was delivered in rail trucks. The train driver would back the full trucks up the line and then leave them there to be unloaded. My job was to move the trucks over the pit and open the gates, sending the grain into the silos. Trouble was, the only way one could move the grain trucks was to ease the brakes off and let it move very, very slowly backwards over the pit. The tracks had a small slope on them so that I didn't have to push and shovel 72 tons of rail truck and grain. All was ok if the brake wasn't let go of! One day the brake wheel didn't stop the rail truck and it kept going until it hit the safety barrier just short of a main road…whew was I lucky!

Working with Darryl on the razor wire was interesting, to say the least. The main jail was a private one. When we arrived every morning we would unload the rolls of wire, all the time being watched by a prison guard with a rifle. Then we would have to wait for clearance to get inside so we could start working. The jail was about two kilometres around its circumference. We would have to push the rolls of wire from the entrance all the way around the outside of the jail, and those rolls were fairly heavy and pushing them that far was really hard work; all the time as we worked up a sweat, I can just remember how Darryl and I were constantly being heckled and jeered at by the prisoners while the prison guard looked on and did nothing. This was a very dangerous job to say the least. Razor wire can cut very deep so I had to be very careful with it, especially when I was inside the roll trying to tie it together. Thankfully I never got cut, but Darryl did a few times. The other big problem with this job was if you needed to go to the toilet. If I was at the far end and I needed to go, I would have to walk two kilometres back to the main entrance, wait ten to fifteen minutes for the guard to let me out and then into the main building's facilities. Then I would have to wait another ten to fifteen minutes for them to come and let me back out again, where I would have to walk the two kilometres back!

CHAPTER THREE

Marriage and Me

I have been married three times. My first marriage was to Denise, the second to Mary-Anne, and the third was to Paula. Each of these ladies are an important part of the overall jigsaw puzzle and each have played an important part in my life. Each relationship had both good and not so good sides to them, but for the most part I have fond memories of each relationship. I think that I get on much better with Denise and Mary-Anne now, however. I will write about Denise first here in Part One, then in Part Two, I will talk about Mary-Anne and Paula.

DENISE

I was married to Denise for twenty-six years and we had four children, all boys: John, Jamie, Daniel and Jeremy.

When I first married Denise we lived with Mum and Dad; then we moved into a little flat and applied for a housing commission house, eventually moving to St Mary's. I joined the Army when I was married to Denise and it was she and John who travelled to Townsville with me. And I was still married to Denise when I first went to University. One night when I was asleep, I woke up around 2am in the morning and went into the kitchen, sat down at the table and just started writing. Then I went back to bed. When I woke up again I went back to see what I had written. It was a poem! Up until this point I did not know that Mum had had her first two children taken from her and did not know that Dad was a stolen child. I have included the poem in the Attachment section.

Jamie, John, me, Daniel and Jeremy at John's wedding.

I have some very fond memories of Denise. She was a nice lady and for the most part we got on well with each other. At some point in our relationship things got a little shaky and then, as relationships sometimes do, things changed. There were many times that Denise would pack my stuff into garbage bags and tell me to get out. I guess we just didn't get on well with each other anymore, and so I felt that I should just do what she wanted and move away. This has never been one of my life's great highlights, but at the time it seemed the best thing to do. We still talk whenever we are in the same company such as family reunions, or a funeral. Denise has a nice fella in her life now and I hope that they have a long and happy time together.

I had a mini-moke when I lived in St Mary's with Denise. It was such a great little car and it would become a favourite of mine. I do remember two specific things that happened when driving it. The moke didn't have a cover on it…it had no roof! But that was the best thing; I loved it most when I would drive in the rain. One day Steve and I were coming back from Parkes and it started pouring down with rain. The thing with the moke was, if it was moving at a reasonable speed you didn't actually get wet. That was, until we had to stop at a set of traffic lights—then we got drenched! The worst time I remember was when I was driving back from Cabramatta. As I was coming to the traffic lights in St Mary's the lights turned red, but as I tried to slow down applying my foot on the brake, it didn't work, and I ran straight into the car in front of me. The other driver hopped out of his car and started yelling at me, but then he looked at his car and the moke. There was much more damage to the moke than the other car; the driver looked back at me but he didn't say anymore, and, deciding he'd gotten the better end of the stick, quickly took off.

I had four sons with Denise. They have been both a blessing and at times a little worrying, but regardless, I love them all.

JOHN

John was the first to be born and it was John who went to Townsville with me. He was such a great baby; he hardly ever got sick, and rarely caused his Mother and I much worry in the early years of his life. John has a huge heart but puts on this other image of himself; I think this is in case he is taken for being something else. He was a good footballer and could run really fast, but he decided not to chase a career in football—and his reasons are his to tell if that's what he wants to do. John is a very hard worker and has a great work ethic. He was a little weird for a time, though. He would go out sometimes and come home when everyone had gone to bed; but he wouldn't knock on the door—instead he would sleep outside under the carport, even in the middle of winter in his shorts and t-shirt. John now has kids of his own and loves having a family of his own.

JAMIE

Jamie was our next child to be born. He was always very strong, physically, and a very outspoken young man when he wanted to be, too. I had a tendency to treat Jamie a little differently from his brothers, but I think this was because he was so outspoken on things that didn't quite sit with what his Mother wanted, or what I needed from him. Jamie has a big heart though and is fun to be with, especially around the campfire we have when we visit Parkes every year. Jamie has a son of his own and I hope that one day he will find his own place in the world and have a good life.

DANIEL

Daniel was our third child to enter into the universe. Daniel, like all his brothers, was fun to have around because he had a sense of mischief about him; I think of all my sons though, Daniel is the most restless. One day I am sure he will find what it is that he wants for himself and his family, as he is now married and has two lovely daughters and a son.

Daniel went to the same University as me, and he eventually found work at the University, too. Daniel is a very good artist. Sometimes he sells his paintings for lots of money—but I think that he doesn't really put the right price on them. I think once he starts to sell more, he may become more confident and lift the prices up a bit.

JEREMY

Next came Jeremy. Jeremy is kind of footloose in that he doesn't really know where he is going or exactly what it is that he wants out of life… he's a little like Daniel and, come to think of it, a little like me when I was younger, I guess. Jeremy had a car accident and was on a life-support system for a while. It was really sad to see him all wired up in the hospital; I will never forget when the neurosurgeon told us that Jeremy only had a few options. What the doctor said was that unless Jeremy was in the lucky 4%, he would not recover and the options presented to us were slim; either we were to leave him in a vegetable state, or make the hardest decision ever to turn off the life support system. These were not very good options!

After talking with his brothers, Denise and I decided as a family that we would wait a few more weeks to see if anything had changed. I remember driving back to Bethanga thinking that there would come a time when I would have to turn the machine off. Miraculously, a few days later Jeremy was awake and asking for the remote for the TV so he could watch football. They were the best words I'd ever heard in my life. Jeremy is now going along really well in life and has children of his own.

I played a lot of golf just around the corner from Grainger Avenue. Sometimes I would take my clubs to work with me and before coming home would play some golf, so I could get much better at it. On some weekends when I played in the local competitions, Jamie and John would caddy for me, which was a big deal for all of us. Funny how they never really took to playing it much though! I do remember however, one day teaching Jeremy how to play. I stood too close to him when he was swinging the club and he accidentally hit me on the side of the face with it and fractured my cheekbone! I also recall the great days we had playing cricket in the backyard. It was always a lot of fun watching the boys pretending to be fast bowlers or terrific batsmen. Lots of tennis balls could be found in the gutters of the neighbour's roof...

All my sons have had some kind of special event/s in their lives and these, I believe, have shaped them into who they are today. I remember the times when I would get them out of bed every Sunday morning and give them a good talking to: a lecture, they called it! I simply wanted what was best for them and I wanted them to be much better than I was, or ever could be. I talked to them about the importance of education, the need for a good work ethic, and the need to give more than they get. I am blessed to have them as my sons, and each of them in their own way has made me very proud of them.

One day I know my time will come to join my Mum and Dad in the spirit world. This to me is simply another piece in the jigsaw puzzle of my life, and is nothing to be afraid of. When that time comes I will always be there for them, looking over them and I will take my father's place as their guardian angel for all the days of their lives. I hope that my sons have grown into the very best people they can be; that they will always be good to their Mother, that they will speak of me fondly and that they will work for their people and their country, so that the name Wiradjuri is not erased historically by the passing of time.

My Brothers and Sisters

Mum with 10 of her 12 children in Parkes for Dad's funeral.

I have spent more of my life with my brothers, rather than my sisters, so my stories are mainly about my brothers! But having said that, both my brothers and sisters are a great comfort to me—though they can also drive me crazy! They all have sons and daughters who also have sons and daughters. Marj is the eldest of us all. Sis is a nice person most of the time and has sometimes had to raise her family under very hard circumstances. They have moved to Parkes and are happy there as family are around them. I had, and still have, issues with the words that she spoke at Mum's funeral service. She told all and sundry that Mum had 10 kids…I was frustrated that she didn't mention the stolen children and felt she should have! I am still very angry with her about this, and it will take a very, very long time to forgive her, if I ever do.

Brother Rob has itchy feet and likes jobs that allow him the opportunity to move around, rather than sit in an office all day. Rob also has children of his own. The problem with Rob is that he hardly does what he says he will do, and even when he gets around to doing something, it takes ages! Darryl moves around a little. At the moment he lives in Bethanga just up the road from where I live. Darryl does mowing and fencing jobs around Bethanga as a way of earning some money. Darryl has two daughters, and they have children of their own too.

Steve is the con-man of my brothers and is always looking for things or ways that can make him rich…but the funny thing is that he is as poor as the rest of us! Steve has children of his own and lives in Parkes. My brother Pete loves the bush, and he is always out fishing or camping, chasing rabbits or getting yabbies. He has children of his own and also lives in Parkes, not very far from Rob or Steve.

My brother Geoff is different from all the others in so many ways, and sometimes I feel as though when he's with family that he doesn't quite fit in, or something like that. Geoff is great, though. He moved to Perth a long time ago and then, yep, you guessed it, he moved to Parkes. After that he moved to Sydney, which is where he still lives today.

Sharry lives on the east coast of NSW after moving away from Parkes. Sharry has children also, but I hardly ever see them. Sis and I never really mixed in the same circles, given the age difference…but we got along ok most of the time.

Ally lives in Queensland and she also has children. I don't get to see her much and I guess most of the time when I do see her it is at family reunions or funerals. Ally is a really, really nice person and I think out of all my brothers and sisters, she would have the biggest heart of them all. Deb lives in Queensland too, not far I think, from her sister Ally. Deb is the female equivalent of Steve…she is/was a big con-woman! She always was a very outspoken woman, but I think she is mellowing with age. All of my brothers and sisters are good people in their own right. They each have done things in their own way, lived where they wanted to, and the way they wanted to, and nearly all have raised family of their own. They have lived good lives. My brothers and sisters, I have realised, are more pieces of the puzzle—and without them the puzzle would not be the same. It's obvious though that most of the antics I got up to were with my brothers.

ROB

I remember a long time ago when Rob and I got into a fight in Cabramatta with some guys. I had fought this guy twice before on the same night, but he came back 'coz he wanted another go at me. There was only me and him—or so I thought. At some point in the fight I found myself lying on the ground; when I looked up, there was this guy about to jump on my head! I couldn't believe it, but there were around twenty guys fighting us now, when I thought that there was only supposed to be the one. We decided to get out of there; as we were running across the street, Rob turned and threw this huge spanner at one of the guys and hit him right smack between the eyes. Rob went one way and I went the other. When I got back to the flat I was living in, there was Rob, unconscious at the top of the stairs. It turned out that one of the guys we were fighting was into karate and had chased Rob down and given him a hiding!

I also remember one day playing football with Rob. He ended up on the sidelines with a broken leg, but I didn't know that at the time.

We were getting beaten badly, yet there on the sidelines was Rob having a smoke, so I walked over and kicked him in the leg thinking he was having a bludge and calling him a bloody bludger! Little did I know I'd just kicked a man with a broken leg! Well, one thing I learned that day about Rob: he can yell really loudly!

DARRYL

When I was working as a furniture removalist, one day I accidentally fell off the back of the truck and broke my wrist and elbow. As I couldn't work and became useless for a while, I decided to go visit Darryl in Narooma where he was living at the time. He suggested that we go prawn fishing because we could sell them and make some money… well, at least it sounded like a good idea. As I had broken bones, Darryl decided that we should make up some kind of sling that would fit over my shoulders so that this way I could drag the net through the water without having to use my bung arm. The water was real muddy, and as a result I lost two pairs of shoes and two pairs of socks because they kept falling off my feet. We dragged the net for ages and got some prawns; at one stage it started to rain and Darryl said we should put on raincoats. Fancy putting a raincoat on when we were already wet and were going back into the water; it made no sense, but that was me! All up, we got enough prawns to make around fifty dollars, which was not a lot, but it did give us some money, and on the plus side we got to eat lots of prawns.

STEVE

Steve usually got on well with everyone, but one day he didn't and he wanted to get back at some guys he didn't like. He invited them to a cards night, and then he invited me too. He told me he was going to rig the games so that he could take all their money. Steve knew how to fix the deck and he told me he would make sure that I won some money, too. But then he took all of my money really early and this put me out of the game. He went on to get the money off the other guys but the greedy bugger didn't give me any! It wasn't a very nice feeling to know I'd been well and truly stiffed, but there you go.

PETE

One day some of the brothers decided to go get some rabbits to eat. The funniest time was when Pete spotted a rabbit, took a shot at it and missed. He was determined to get the rabbit, so Pete jumped off the ute chasing after it, but the rabbit turned around and ran up the dirt track. Well, it was winter time and Pete had lots of clothes on to keep warm, plus a huge army coat over the top of all that. So now here was Pete, running up the road chasing this rabbit, both of them at full speed! When the rabbit got to the top of the hill, it turned around and ran right back down towards us again. So Pete, in hot pursuit, did the same thing. When the rabbit got back to the ute (which was loaded full of guys all laughing at what was happening), it turned around to see where Pete was and whack! The rabbit hit the fence post and knocked itself out! It was the funniest thing we'd seen for a very long time.

SOME FRIENDS

I have met many people over the years and some of them have remained very good friends. Jon Pearse (Pinhead), Desi Ingram (Beachball), Bruce Leverton (Snakey), and Steve Kemp (Kempy) were among my best friends. I have been blessed with the comings and goings of these different people and they have had some influence in what I have done, and what I would eventually do in my life.

Jon, Steve and Bruce.

Jon (Pinhead) and I both worked at a University as cleaners, and after that we both worked together on the railway, then we had the dog food business together. Going into business with Jon was great fun. We would get broken bags of dog and cat food from a factory and take them home so we could put them in new bags and sell them at the markets. We would mix the stuff together in the bathtub with a spade. We got into lots of trouble from the wives for doing that, because the spade left huge scratches in the bath! I'm reminded that my sons helped out here a lot, too. They would help mix the dog food and also help me load the car with the bags and assist me in selling it at the markets.

Bruce is like family to me as we grew up with him, and Mum and Dad got on well with him too. In the early years though, Bruce spent more time with Rob. Bruce would do anything for the family and I remember that my sons have each been given a twenty-first birthday pewter mug to commemorate this milestone. One day after golf, Bruce called and asked if I wanted a lift home. He picked me up around 9am in the morning—and it was nearly midnight when I eventually had to telephone home for someone to come and get me! Bruce had this habit of not being able to get from point A to point B without going in a crooked line. Bruce was always his own person and could be very forthright in saying what was on his mind. Sometimes he didn't think before he said anything though, and this always got him offside with people. Bruce has since passed away, but he was always a loyal and good friend to me.

Steve is a really great fella. He got on well with Mum and Dad because he was always respectful around them. I remember one year going away on a football trip. Desi had suggested that we play touch football in the backyard of the pub, but touch football quickly turned to tackle, and during the game Steve broke his ankle and we had to take him to hospital. He decided that he would never play football again, but we eventually talked him around a few years later after he had healed.

Desi always had time for me regardless of what I needed from him or what I asked him to do. It was Desi who played Santa Claus for the family one year, and for this I will be eternally grateful because it was the last Christmas that the family would get to spend with Nan and Pop. It was Desi's idea to play Santa Claus that year and he arrived all dressed up as Santa, so I took him up the road on the bonnet of the car. I drove him back down the street and all the kids from all the houses came out to see Santa Claus, and Desi gave them all packets of lollies. There were at least two hundred presents under the tree that year because all the family were there. Desi started handing out the presents and when it came to Pop's present, he didn't know who 'Albert' was so he just called out, "present for Albert Namatjirra!" This caused so much laughter that we all had tears in our eyes! One of the little ones wanted to know how come Santa was white. I couldn't answer that one. But we had the best Christmas ever and it was all because of my friend, Desi.

PART
TWO

CHAPTER FIVE

The Birth of Yalmambirra

Yalmambirra was born in the year 1997. This all happened because of the information told to me by my Mother, following Dad's passing away. Mum had told me that Dad was a stolen child, stolen from his natural family when he was just a youngster. This was also when Mum told me that her first two children, too, had been stolen. The many First Nations children who had been forcibly removed from their families as a result of the government's policies between 1910-1970 became known as the Stolen Generation, and has left behind a long legacy of trauma in its wake. This was very sad, and I thought long and hard about what I could or should do. As I was living in Albury at the time I decided to speak to my most senior Wiradjuri Elder, and he offered some advice after I told him what I was thinking of doing.

I wanted to change my name because I no longer wanted anything to do with a white name, especially since it was the white man who had had something to do with taking and keeping my father from his true family. They wrongly thought that by assimilating the children of Aboriginal and Torres Strait Islander people into white society that they would improve their lives, allowing the race to slowly "die out" by the process of natural elimination. They were taught to reject their Indigenous heritage, and forced to adopt white culture. Names were often changed, and many were forbidden from speaking traditional languages. Some children were adopted by white families, and many more were placed in institutions where abuse and neglect were common. The resulting intergenerational trauma has had a marked impact on the first peoples of this land and has severely disrupted the passing on of my culture and cultural knowledge, which risks being lost forever for having lain dormant so long. When I explained this to my Elder, he suggested a name for me, along with advice and instructions on what I should do. I was to speak with all my family and let them know how I felt, and that I wanted to change my name. Should any of my brothers or sisters or Mum, say no, then I would not be able to go ahead with it. Thankfully no one objected and so I went ahead with my name change, but some family members did say that they thought changing my name would then be considered disrespectful to Dad. This made me kind of angry because what they didn't understand was that it was the complete opposite! However, I still did not know what name the Elder had chosen for me at the time and I had to wait to find out.

Eventually, I spoke again with the Elder and he said that the name he had chosen for me was Yalmambirra, which means to 'teach, speak.' He told me that he had given me this name because he thought I would become a great teacher. I thanked him and told him I was very happy with the name Yalmambirra. The Elder then introduced me to the Wiradjuri Council of Elders and suggested that I join. It was a really great experience meeting with, and getting knowledge from, the Elders because it helped me reconnect with my heritage and my roots. This senior Wiradjuri Elder has since passed into the spirit world and I will always be very, very grateful for all his help and knowledge. His sister

Aunty Flo ran the Council of Elders after her brother passed away, but sadly, Aunty Flo has also now gone to the spirit world.

Cec and Flo with a little Jacob

THE ALBURY EXPERIENCES

I went to University in Albury and became a student because of Rob. He was already a student and told me that I should go to University as well. There was this program that the Wiradjuri people could go into to see if they were suited for University, and so Rob dared me to enter the program—then he made me promise that if I passed that first test, I would see the degree through. Well, I thought; how on earth was I going to pass anything when I didn't have any education to speak of! I passed though, and it was the happiest day when I got accepted into Charles Sturt University in Albury.

Me and Rob on the day I applied to come to Uni.

When I moved from Sydney to Albury, I found a small flat to live in. It didn't have any furniture in it and, as I didn't have a job at the time, the idea of paying bills wasn't really all that great of an idea to me, and so I got the gas heating turned off and for the first two winters slept only on a towel in my clothes on the floor. Eventually, I bought a bed and some linen and slowly I began to settle in properly.

I met some really nice people in Albury and most were to become great friends of mine; to this day they are still my friends, even if I haven't seen them for a while. Shaun is a really great guy; he can be outspoken at times but he has this weird sense of humour! But Shaun looked after me and showed me the pitfalls of University life and helped me develop my research skills. He is married to a very nice lady called Rochelle, who is always very respectful and very kind to me. For a few years in a row we would travel up to the Buckland River at Easter time and camp out. It was really great fun until Mary-Anne got bitten by a very large ant!

Shaun and Rochelle at the campsite in the Buckland River.

Ben was to become a good friend too, and he eventually became my boss! Ben can also be outspoken and he also has a weird sense of humour, but Ben has been the driving force behind all the desert trips that I have been on.

In my time at University, I have met literally thousands of people. I have met these people in the halls of academia, in the classrooms, at conferences, and on desert trips. These people are all pieces of my jigsaw puzzle, with a lot of them still very close friends of mine.

In the year 2000, I decided to apply for funding to revegetate the Mungabareena Reserve into something that it may have been like, before weed infestation and unwanted human interaction turned it into an area that people didn't want to visit anymore.

An information sign along with a Murray cray that had been washed up in flood waters.

I was walking around the Reserve with Cec, my senior Wiradjuri Elder, when we suddenly heard a big scream! A little girl on a school excursion had come face to face with a very large cow! We decided then and there that the cows should go so that people could use the Reserve for recreational purposes and not have to worry about the cows. With help from Ben and Jess, I applied to the Natural Heritage Trust for funding and was successful to the tune of, I think, $11,700. This funding provided us the opportunity to get rid of the weeds, open up some of the walking tracks and revegetate the area.

I approached Albury City Council for help and they carried out a controlled burning of the area. Then I contacted some schools in the area to see if they would allow school children to come out and plant some trees. Around 500 school children turned up over this period of planting. I held barbecues to feed the kids but was warned not to give them red cordial. They drank about fifty litres of red cordial, and as a result of this, around 11,400 native trees and shrubs and wetland grasses were planted very quickly by a lot of kids high on sugary red juice!

A problem arose when the Albury Council didn't want to stop the cattle agistment, and so I put a fence up around the planting area so the cows couldn't get in and eat the plants. Little did I know that would be when the trouble started! The fence was cut, and after spending two days fixing it, again it was cut. After fixing it, again it was cut, and now about thirty metres of the fencing had been thrown in the Murray River. I pulled it out and fixed it up. Then the gate was stolen! Then it rained and rained and rained. A big flood came through and pushed some of the fencing over and covered most of it with debris. It was all a shambles. I asked the Council to stop the agistment, and to their credit, they did so. Now I could take the fence down. But soon, more trouble followed. Some of the plants were stolen and many more had been destroyed, by four-wheel-drive vehicles driving over them. The trouble only continued; some of the picnic tables were stolen, then signs were torn down and run over. When the school children had helped in the planting, I had promised them that I would put their names on a plaque so they could bring their Mums and Dads down to have a look at all the plants they had put in. There were five hundred names on that plaque; sadly, after a few weeks, the plaque was stolen.

Mungabareena Reserve is now registered as an Aboriginal Place and, as such, is now controlled by a working group of mostly Wiradjuri peoples, young and old; they operate under specific legal guidelines to preserve this sacred land, and I believe that soon the Reserve will be rehabilitated once again.

THE WIRADJURI PEOPLES

When I first learned of the secrets my parents had held from me, I immediately thought, "I'm Wiradjuri and I've got to do something about this." I just had to know who I was and where I had come from.

Now, with the help of the Elders who had imparted their wisdom and knowledge to me, along with my new name Yalmambirra, I was hungry to learn more. Drawing on thousands of old diaries, notebooks and literature, written largely from a colonist's perspective, my research began, and I started to explore the challenges of Wiradjuri culture, and the things they faced, because they had previously only ever been documented as inferior and stone-age. For example, many of the books I read as part of my research suggested that Wiradjuri peoples were cannibals. This set me on a path to interviewing over forty Wiradjuri people from across Wiradjuri country, asking about their cultural background and knowledge. My interviews touched on the Stolen Generations, their dispossession and relocation to missions and reserves. I wanted to learn more about the impact of government policies and how contemporary policies define Indigenous people today.

There was so much I needed to learn; yet it seemed the more I learned the less I felt I knew! The Wiradjuri peoples were the largest language group in New South Wales; they were unique in that they had their own language and were united by a common language, along with strong ties of kinship. They survived as skilled hunter–fisher–gatherers in family groups or clans scattered throughout central New South Wales and west of the Blue Mountains in an area known as "the three rivers." There were several other tribes to the west of the Great Dividing Range that were similarly named after their own words for "no," but Wiradjuri remained the largest language group. Today, the Wiradjuri language was effectively extinct, but attempts are underway to revive it with a reconstructed grammar, based on earlier ethnographic materials and wordlists and the memories of Wiradjuri families, which is now used to teach the language in schools. These carvings were demonstrated proof of their notable artistic power. Then came the Bathurst Wars in 1824, which resulted in the occupation of their lands, and the cultivation of the influx of whites, causing famine in the Wiradjuri peoples, eventually driving them out. Governor Lachlan Macquarie wrote of the Wiradjuri people:

"We found here also three male natives and four boys of this newly
discovered tract of country, who showed great surprise,
mixed with no small degree of fear, at seeing so many strangers,
horses and carriages but to whom they soon appeared to be reconciled on being kindly spoken to.
They were all clothed with Mantles made of the skins of o'possums
which were neatly sewn together and the outside of the skins were carved in a remarkably neat manner.
They appear to be very inoffensive and cleanly in their persons."

CHAPTER SIX

Ladies That I Know

At this point in time, I have only three very, very special ladies in my life: Jodie, Jennifer and Miranda. I do have lady friends like Lee's wife, Jackie, or Greg's wife, Sandra, for example—but Jodie, Jennifer and Miranda are different.

JODIE

Jodie is a very special lady. I first met her when I was teaching at Charles Sturt University and she graduated in the year 2002. Jodie has a very distinctive outlook on life and I guess this is why I like her as much as I do. She was so very excited when she shared with me the recent discovery of her ancestral Native American heritage. It always seemed to me that we just naturally understood each other, and Jodie has always made me smile. Jodie once gave me a very beautiful chalk pastel drawing of a kangaroo's face (my totem), and it takes pride of place in my dining room.

Jodie loves this part of Wiradjuri Country, and I know she misses it. Jodie loved living and studying on Wiradjuri lands; Country still calls her back every now and then. I remember Jodie as a student; she always turned up to class passionate to learn all she could about Indigenous cultures, and how to engage with community and look after Country. When walking on Country, she would always ask me questions and wanted to learn as much as she could. She made me feel special as a teacher and as an Elder of my community. The photo below shows me and Jodie on her graduation day.

JENNIFER

Jennifer is a former student of mine who graduated in the year 2012 and lives in Queensland. We haven't seen each other for years and years but we email, phone and write letters to each other so we don't lose touch. Jennifer is such a great lady; unfortunately she has a form of brain damage, but this does not restrict her from doing things like fundraising and trekking long distances for her causes. Jennifer has a penchant for writing short stories. One short story she wrote was about an old dingo (Warrigal) wanting to go home, and it was such a great read that I have continued to work with Jennifer to have it illustrated and published. Jennifer also does some really weird, and wonderful videos that she puts online so people can see them. I really hope that Jennifer and I can catch up with each other soon. That would be terrific.

Jennifer: Pausing for breath on one of her many treks.

MIRANDA

I call Miranda 'Stunner' because she is such a stunningly attractive lady, with a smile that melts my heart. Stunner is also a former student of mine and she graduated in 2007 with an Honours degree. She is the Mother of two great kids: Cameron and Sari. Little Sari got really sick and had to go into hospital, but thankfully she recovered and is now back home. Stunner went on one of the desert trips with me and she was so much fun to have in the ute. It was Stunner who introduced me to the music by Deep Forest, which is really cool stuff, and when I play this music (which is often), it brings back memories of her sitting in the back seat smiling with her headphones on. I couldn't help but keep looking in the rear vision mirror that day. We always kept in touch though, and it was always great to chat with her and talk about things. One day when I was living at Bethanga, she asked if she could come down and stay with me for a few days; it was great to have her there and we had a good time, but of course she had to eventually go home.

It was a few years later when Stunner asked if she could visit me again. This time I was in the new house in Lavington, and of course, I said "yes!" We went driving around and visiting different places and I had such a fantastic time during those very short few days with her. I felt very, very sad when it was time for Stunner to leave and I had to take her back to the airport; sad, because I had a feeling that I would never see her again. Just as well I'm really great at technology (ha!), so now I can 'text' her! But Stunner has this habit of taking ages to text me back. She had to go to Coffs Harbour as her Grandma was ill. Whilst she was there, her Grandma passed away and I know it is very hard for her at the moment. I hope she will be ok real soon.

Miranda.

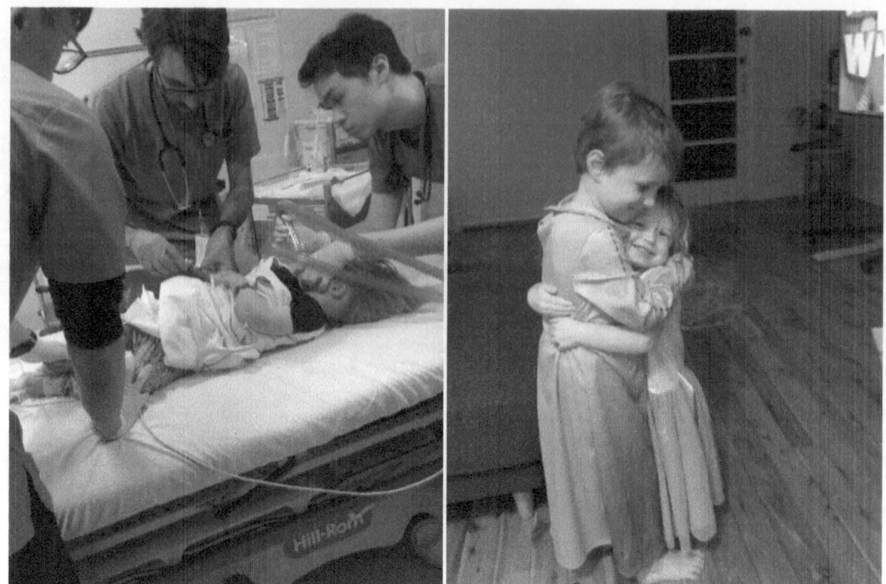

A very sick Sari and a big welcome home from Cameron.

UNIVERSITY LIFE

I was on the dole when I moved to Albury, but all that changed in the year of 1997. I used the Indigenous Education Centre as a base from which to do my studies and in 1997, I looked after the centre when the two people that worked there went on holidays. I was allowed to look at the faxes that came through in case something urgent came up; then, one day a fax came through that was to change my life in so many ways.

The fax was asking the centre's staff if they knew anyone who could teach Indigenous studies to students. I kept the fax and waited until the holidays were over; then I went to see the lady who had sent it. Within ten minutes I had signed a contract to become a University lecturer! And I was still a student! Now I could get the gas turned on and buy some furniture! In time I was asked to apply for the position as the Koori Academic at the University for the School of Environmental Science. I applied for the position and was given the job on a two-year contract.

So now here I was, a student and a lecturer at the same time, and believe me, it was really hard trying to juggle both. I got my degree, a Bachelor of Applied Science, and then my contract ran out. The photo below shows Pete, me, Darryl and Rob on my graduation day.

The University offered me the position again on the condition that I undertake a higher degree. This time I studied for an Honours degree. At the end of all my hard work I received a Class 1 Honours degree, which was really great. Then the contract ran out again! This time the University told me that I could have the job again on tenure, if I agreed to undertake a higher degree research project. I agreed; this time I did my PhD. I completed the PhD after around eleven years of gruelling work and study. There were times when outside influences detracted from my studies and this set me back a fair bit, but in the end I completed it, and I was awarded my PhD in 2013.

In my time at University I have written a number of papers and had some of them published. Most have as their main theme, issues that are relevant to Wiradjuri peoples, cultures and country, and a list of them can be found at the end of the book.

Also during my years at University, I had the pleasure of going on what we called 'the desert trip.' Ben was the instigator of these outback adventures, and one day at the pub, he and Shaun asked me to go on one of the trips. At first I said "no," but they got me a little tipsy and then I signed the paperwork. My job on the trips was to drive the backup vehicle, get the fire going, and cook dinner. There was lots of stuff to do, but I loved it!

Cooking by colour coding, for 20 people on one of the trips.

The desert trips were such fun, and every trip was different from the last one. For most of the time, the students were really great and I made some good friends, friends that I still have today. Each desert trip threw up something that tested us as a group. I remember them all, but a few really stand out.

One trip saw two girls get very sick and we were actually thinking of flying them out to a hospital so they could be cared for. Mootawingee National Park was one place where we used to camp. I gave a little cultural talk to the students and warned them about taking things from places such as these.

Giving a cultural lesson in the desert.

When we were setting up camp, one of the students came over with some rocks that she had picked up. I had to tell her to put them back as some of them were artefacts. About ten minutes later she came back with some more! This time I had to tell her more sternly to put them back; she started to cry, but she put them back. Then when we got to Arkaroola a few days later where we were going to camp, I noticed that the oil in the bus was leaking out. The first thing to do, however, was to put the two sick girls into a cabin so they were more comfortable.

Ben and I asked the mechanic if he could fix the bus but he said he couldn't do it for another three days. At around 6am the next day, Ben woke everyone up. He said to the students to put their hands up if they had any rocks. Hands went up everywhere! We collected lots of rocks, put them into a bag and stored them in a box under the front seat of the bus. When Ben and I went to check on the girls, they were up, dressed and ready for the tour. There wasn't anything wrong with them. Thankfully, the mechanic had fixed the bus overnight! Ben sent the rocks back to National Parks people, as there were artefacts among the rocks that had been taken that needed to be returned.

On another trip the same thing happened: students picked up the rocks! When I drove the backup ute I would stay about five kilometres behind the bus; this was because of the amount of dust coming from the bus, and most times I couldn't see the road if I drove any closer. I came around a corner and saw that the bus had pulled over to the side of the road. All the students were getting off the bus and they were all covered in red dust. Then Shaun got out of the driver's seat and he was covered in red dust. It appeared that the bus had hit a rock, then the rock hit the front of the trailer which then hit the back windscreen of the bus, smashing it! We had to kick the windscreen out and tape a tarp over it. This wasn't very effective, however, so we had to tape all the little nooks and crannies, and that seemed to work much better.

In all the desert trips that I had been on, we never had a real bad accident. But on one particular trip we had, that was all about to change. Ben had decided that we were going to take another route back, and so down the dirt road we went. Again, I drove about five kilometres behind; that was when I saw the bus coming the other way. Ben had missed the turn-off. I waited for a little while so the bus could get ahead of us. Then I drove slowly, as the road we were on was very hard to drive on. I saw a spare wheel on the side of the road, so I stopped to pick it up, because it looked like the spare from the bus. Just as I reached fourth gear, I heard a noise, and the ute came to a dead halt. Dust went everywhere. Paula was in the front seat and her legs slammed into the dashboard, and the student in the back seat was thrown forward. Good thing we were all wearing seatbelts!

We got out and saw that the trailer had flipped over and was now lying on its side in the dust. The first thing I could smell was the gas, then I saw that the diesel drums were also leaking. I told the student to start the distress beacon and then told Paula to walk to the top of the hill and stop any traffic coming over the hill. We were now lying across the road and it was a dangerous situation. I got the fuel cans off the trailer and opened the door and saw that the gas bottles had been turned on. I started to clean up and clean out the trailer because it was just a huge mess inside of it. A ute came down the road and thankfully he had some chains, so we managed to turn the trailer upright onto its wheels again and drove it off the road.

Then Ben and the bus came over the hill and he saw what had happened. I asked Ben what he had thought when he saw us and the mess; he said he just wanted to count people, and was relieved to see that we were all accounted for and walking around and safe. I did get into trouble for having the beacon on, though. Ben had to call Canberra so they didn't send out a search plane! Then when everything was ok again, I was driving back up to the turnoff and the bus had stopped again; I saw Ben get out and start looking under the trailer. The shackles holding the wheel axle onto the trailer had come loose! Gotta love those desert trips!

I liked working at the University. I especially liked the classes, and for the most part the students were really great and wanted to learn about Aboriginal cultures and peoples. One year I decided to put my teaching and the students' learning to the test. I found a venue that could hold all of my students and lots of children at the same time. I asked the students to put together some activities that they wanted to teach the children. I divided the class into groups and they had their own area in which to present their activities to the children. This was a huge success and so I ran the same platform for around five years. At one stage I counted over four hundred children aged from five years old to high school students, all at the one session! It was a huge success and I received the team teaching award for doing so well, which was a really great achievement and one of my career highlights to date.

MY PHD THESIS, "INDIGENOUS CULTURES IN CONTEMPORARY AUSTRALIA: A WIRADJURI CASE STUDY."

I was awarded my PhD titled "Indigenous Cultures in Contemporary Australia: A Wiradjuri Case Study" during a ceremony in Albury in December, 2015. I went on to become an Elder in Residence at CSU in Albury-Wodonga, lecturing in Indigenous studies and Indigenous land management.

My PhD was designed around two things: to provide an avenue where Wiradjuri peoples could have a voice, and to show the broader Australian community that we are still here, that we haven't gone away and we are just as valid now as we were 120,000 years ago.

"In order to understand where people are today you need to be able to understand where they were in the past."

I have now turned my research into a text in the hopes that this will help students better understand our history and Wiradjuri culture. I think it is so important that the voices of those 41 Wiradjuri people I interviewed are taken into consideration when these students read the published historical narratives of Indigenous peoples and culture. I must say I am not an advocate for burning the books. I think all of those resources that I used for my research are very important because they portray an Australia that is out of line with First Nations' peoples. And I think people need to read those books to put what we say into perspective. It's up to people to make up their own mind. We plant little seeds and how they nurture those seeds is entirely up to them.

I still find it funny to think that my whole educational journey at CSU began on a dare, and I have Rob to thank for it—because he was the one who that day planted a seed. I really was a bad bugger when I was young and I had no educational background; my only education came from my workmates, who were much older than me. Rob went on to graduate from CSU too, with a Bachelor of Parks, Recreation and Heritage in 1995. So I guess you could say that it was Rob who set me on a new life path; and this would become yet another piece in the jigsaw puzzle of Yalmambirra.

Mary-Anne

Mary-Anne with Jacob

I met Mary-Anne at a meeting and was immediately taken by her demeanour; the way she talked, held herself, and of course, the way she looked, all spoke to me. A few days after the meeting I asked her out and she said "yes!" After a few dates we found we got on really well and decided that we could live together, so we decided to do something about it. Mary-Anne had her own house and I was living in my flat, so I gave up the flat and moved into Amatex Street in East Albury, where she lived. The problem was that Mary-Anne was working in Canberra at the time, so it still felt as though as I was living on my own sometimes. I used to drive up to Canberra to see her for the weekend and sometimes she would come down to Albury, and that was how we made it work. We never really spent that much time together in the early days, I guess.

Mary-Anne got a job in Albury and so she moved back into her house and things were going along really well. We decided that we would like to move, so we started looking around at a few houses; this led to us buying up twenty acres of land, and we found a builder called Michael Taylor who said he would help us build our own house. Mick was already building our neighbour's, Jon and Joan's house next door, which was where we found him.

Jon and Joan with Jacob

Mick was really great, and once the house was designed, he built something really special for us. I think that our home was the last building that Mick ever built commercially.

Preparing the building site.

Mary-Anne then got pregnant with Jacob around the time we were moving. At one stage we were actually living in three places at the same time, which was a bit much. I stayed in Amatex Street to finish cleaning up and moving furniture, while Mary-Anne moved into a rented house with Jacob where he was born, and I sometimes slept at the property. When the house was finally built, we were all together again and had a good time planting trees and doing things around the property to make it more comfortable for us.

Things appeared to be going along ok for a while, but some things started changing, and some of these changes I didn't see coming. When things got worse between us, we decided to separate. This separation eventually led to our divorce, which was a traumatic time for both of us. I moved out as I didn't want Mary-Anne and Jacob having to find another place to live and having to become destitute. After a period at attempted reconciliation (which didn't work), Mary-Anne decided to move from the property and get a place closer to Albury. I wanted to keep the property and so we came to an agreement that was beneficial to both of us.

Sometimes relationships work and sometimes they don't; what I have learned is that when a relationship finishes, it hurts, and then the hurt goes away and one just learns to move on, just as Mary-Anne and I have done. We get on now, it appears, much better being apart than being married. We chat about different things and Mary-Anne has a new fella, which is great for her and for Jacob. I am very happy that things have worked out for both of them.

JACOB

The youngest of all my sons, Jacob, was born Jacob Gindhay Scully. He too is a Wiradjuri boy and his spiritual connection to his ancestors and to Wiradjuri country is through his totem, which is dinawaan, the emu.

Jacob with dinawaan, the emu.

Jacob was such a great little baby and we never had any problems at all with him. He was always smiling and always very, very happy and we had such wonderful times together. There are so many memories of Jacob that it is hard for me to choose only some for my story, but here are some.

There was a time when Jacob had to go into hospital for an eye operation and his Mother was crying, and he was crying and that upset me a lot, but into the operating room they wheeled him anyway. We waited for what seemed like ages and then we heard this great piercing scream and the doctors let Mary-Anne in to try and calm him down! He was still screaming when they wheeled him out into the recovery room. He quietened down though, when the nurse brought him some vegemite sandwiches and a great big bowl of custard…it worked and he ate the lot!

After a while Jacob settled down and I remember we were playing with some toys when the nurse came in, announcing that soon Jacob could go home. I'll never forget seeing little Jacob's round face and big eyes look up at me as he said "Home." He wanted to go home! It nearly brought tears to my eyes. Then the nurse said that there was one more test that they needed to do, and Jacob turned and yelled "Noooo!" My son understood exactly what was happening around him.

As Jacob grew, so did his personality. He had his own way of doing things and his own way of getting around anything that presented him with a challenge. Jacob's mind developed really quickly and I was always baffled by his language skills; I couldn't understand what it was that he was saying, but he certainly did. I especially liked it when he played with his train because it always seemed to come apart, and then he would bring it over to me, saying "Your turn, Daddy's turn." This always meant that he wanted me to fix it for him, but when I wanted a turn he would protest, saying, "No, my turn, my turn!" I couldn't help but think he was turning into a little con-man just like his Uncle Steve!

When Jacob's Mother brought him for a visit he would always ask if he could have a lolly. He would say, "Lolly, one, one lolly," and hold up one finger. Then of course it went from one lolly to "two lollies." He was a tough negotiator and knew how to get what he wanted!

Caught with his hands in the lolly jar!

Jacob liked sitting in the ute with me and pretending that he was driving it. When he wanted me to take him for a drive, he would open the door, move over to the passenger's side and put the seatbelt on! I got Jacob a little dog and we called it Migay, which is Wiradjuri for girl.

Jacob's friend Migay.

One day, Jacob thought that Migay would like to go for a drive too, and he said, "Migay, Migay in ute."

Jacob is a very physical kid. He has often told me that he wants to be a pilot. He has already flown a plane with other passengers when he was on holidays in Queensland. Jacob likes sailing too, but he has put his sail boat up for sale, as he now has his boat license so he helps out on the rescue boat. In one day, he rescued five people, amongst them, was his Mother! He also loves cross-country skiing with his Mother and they go up to Falls Creek most weekends in winter as Mary-Anne has joint ownership at an on-site caravan park in Mt Beauty, which means they don't have to book accommodation and can virtually come and go whenever they want. It was Mary-Anne who first introduced me to cross-country skiing. It wasn't that bad, but I'm not really a skier! Jacob has now decided he wants to be a photographer and has a really great camera and has even had an exhibition where he sold some of his works. Hang on…now he wants to be an electrician!

Me: Looks the part...but can't ski!

It is vitally important to me that Jacob learns all he can about his history, Wiradjuri history. For our cultures to survive into the next 120,000 years we need young people such as Jacob to learn the stories and the ways of being and doing that are inherent in being Wiradjuri. There will be many stories that Jacob will be told and many of them will be sad stories. He will feel any number of emotions from despair and frustration to anger; but what has been done has been done. What is more important is that the truth be told, and the way for Jacob and others like him to ensure that they don't happen again, is to pass the messages on generationally. He and others like him must take Wiradjuri forward. This is a huge load to bear, but I believe Jacob will grow into a very, very strong person and I am sure that he will do what is right and do so with humility, pride and confidence. Jacob is part of the Nation of Wiradjuri and a part of one of the oldest living cultures in the world. He, like all Wiradjuri, is unique!

PAULA

I first met Paula at University during what is called a residential school. I was her lecturer and we had emailed each other a number of times about her assignments and other course work. Not for one minute did I think that I would have a relationship with her. Paula lived in a suburb of Melbourne and I used to drive down there to see her and she would drive up to see me. Paula wanted to leave her job, and so we thought she should move in with me on the property. That led to us making the decision to get married. Paula was a very attractive person and I liked the way she liked and loved me.

I remember lots of things about Paula. I think that she always 'timed' me when I was having a shower. I would be in the middle of showering and she would yell out "two minutes are up!" Paula finished her degree at the University and was excited about graduating. I remember that I told her that I would make mention during my Welcome to Country of the fact that my wife was graduating that day. She became very adamant that I was not to do that. Bad physical things would happen to me if I said anything! So I kept quiet and things went smoothly and she looked great in her graduation gown. I was so very, very proud of my Paula.

Paula had two horses: Pearl and Ava. One day she decided to wash Pearl. We had put the water tank on the ute and tied the horse to the back of the ute. That way she could wash the horse and the horse would not be able to run off or play up. Wrong! Everything was going along ok and for a time both Paula and Pearl looked like they were having fun. Then as Paula was moving under the horse's neck it fell over and landed on her. I thought she was squashed! When the horse got back to its feet, Paula got up off the ground and although very wet and muddy, she was all right. I had thought she had been very seriously hurt. She never washed Pearl that way again!

At one point in time, Paula decided to get some chickens. I don't really have anything good to say about them. When I would mow the lawn they would follow the mower and eat the bugs that jumped out of the grass. One day one of the chickens went in front of the mower and disappeared in front of my eyes. I stopped the mower, got off to have a look and to my surprise the chicken was still alive but the mower wheel was on the chicken's neck! After I let it go, it never followed me again. Being the smart person that I am, I never told Paula about it. One day when I was in the pub, Paula called me to say that she wanted me to come home. She was crying and couldn't tell me what was wrong. When I got home, Paula was still crying and all she could do was point out to the front yard. There were chicken feathers everywhere and the thing was dead! Paula wanted me to move the chicken and pick up the feathers so she couldn't see them again. Then, she said, she could stop crying.

Paula had a pet rabbit called Smidge. It was actually very well behaved and would come when called. But it was getting on in years and one day it got really sick and she took it to the vet. Smidge didn't survive the surgery and died. This was a very sad time for Paula, as she loved that rabbit a lot. I buried Smidge the rabbit on the property and put a little wooden cross next to it. Horses, chickens, and Smidge. What more could she want? A dog! Paula decided that she wanted a dog. She came home one day with a German Shepherd pup and she called it Elsa. Paula wanted to have the dog trained and so she took it to doggy school every now and then, and as time went by Elsa became a much better behaved dog, which was good. Paula had a big heart when it came to animals and she seemed to have a really good way with them, and they responded to her really well too.

After about two years of marriage, things changed between us. I found myself arguing with Paula more and more; even now, looking back, I am not really sure why, or what over. And so I found myself on my own again as Paula had decided to move out and return to Melbourne. Funny thing though, because when Paula was living there she wanted a pond for the horses and she wanted me to stop spending all my time at the pub; when things started going bad, Paula asked that I sell girragirra ganya and move with her elsewhere. In the end I put in the ponds, stopped drinking at the pub and eventually sold, not even thinking that we had actually discussed any of it. Even though there were some really great times with Paula, there were some really bad ones, too. When Paula moved out she went and saw some solicitors—and then she told me she wanted a financial settlement. Then she got her Solicitors to put a 'caveat' on the property! This meant that I was not allowed to do any development work or sell the property. If I didn't pay her the money then they would sell the property, pay Paula, and then I would get the rest. Paula has not told me where in Melbourne she lives, but I eventually managed to contact her by letter. She wrote back saying that she wouldn't phone or write, and so I will not have any further contact with her. I emailed Paula in relation to including her in the book. Paula replied to my email which was really great!

CHAPTER EIGHT

Life Goes On

Every year the boys all get together for a golf and bowls weekend in memory of Dad in Parkes. Life for family is going along ok. Three of my brothers came down for a visit last Easter to have a chat about the coming October.

Remembering Dad on Parkes golf course.

I am hoping that the girls in the family do something special for Mum every year in memory of her, too. Deb and Ally still live in Queensland, Marj and her family have settled back into Parkes, Sharry still lives on the coast, Darryl still lives in Bethanga, and Daniel is happy with his new job and is thinking about moving into a bigger house as the girls and Archie are getting older and need more room. My sons are all going along ok and each is living their own life with their own families. Sometimes I catch up with them, but not enough times, though.

I am now retired from work. I don't like being retired, but I survive. I spend most of my time working on the property and making it more comfortable and more presentable should it come to the stage where I cannot look after it anymore and decide to sell it. That will be a very sad day indeed. I live on my own since Paula left in 2013 and I don't think that I will ever have someone else in my life again. I just have to make the best of it, I guess.

My life at Bethanga is ok. Darryl had moved to Bethanga and rented a house just down the road from me. He got a job in Lavington as a groundsman cleaning and mowing and keeping the caravan park nice and neat. He also mows lawns around Bethanga for some people and always does a great job. I have met some really nice people, the likes of Lee, Gazza, Jon, Andrew, Pete, Greg and Pup, and their friendship is a great comfort to me. They too, have all become pieces of the jigsaw puzzle.

I guess that I have more interaction with the guys than I do the ladies, but Lee's wife Jackie is a really nice person and she has never been disrespectful to me and always greets me with a smile whenever I drop in to see them. Greg's wife Sandra is also a very nice person. Sandra is always willing to give me some tips on gardening, which comes in very handy. Both Jackie and Sandra are part of the connections that I will always have with Bethanga.

Jackie and Lee

Lee and I play golf sometimes—not enough though! But when we do find the time to play, we have a great time. Lee has a driveway that I call the 'driveway of death!' One wrong move and into the wall or over the edge you go! We even bought our own golf cart. Well, the batteries in the golf cart shit themselves and then it cost $2000 to replace all six of them! We need to use it more to justify its cost, which means more golf, unfortunately…ha!

Gazza is the one friend out of all of them who has the weirdest sense of humour. He is very dry! Gazza has helped me to build things on the property, and likes to scare the jirri jirri's and magpies. Gazza doesn't like snakes and twice they have scared him to death! On one occasion Gazza decided to have a pee next to the trailer. Next thing he screamed—yep, screamed—and then he jumped about ten feet in the air! I went over to see what was the matter and there on the ground was a brown snake with a rat in its mouth. Gazza had peed on it!

Then another time Gazza and I were just sitting in front of the shed having a beer and hanging out; I was looking at the ants on the ground when I heard Gazza suddenly yell out. I looked around and his legs were up in the air. A black snake had gone under his chair and between his legs! The snake came over to me, had a look at me then slithered past, disappearing around the side of the shed. He didn't bother me one bit. All I saw was a snake doing his thing, while I was doing my thing. It took a while for Gazza to sit back down in that chair again.

Gazza played me in darts at the pub one night and beat me! Now he won't play me again because he reckons he doesn't have anything to prove. He also beat me in pool and yep, same thing again, he won't play me for the same reason as he won't play me in darts again. Makes no sense to me, he should be feeling good because he won.

Jon has the property next door and I first met him when we were both studying at University. He has lots of cows and I have leased my hay paddock to him so he can have some extra feed for them. Andrew lives about an hour's drive down the road and I used to catch up with him at the pub. He once tricked some guys into believing he had a crocodile in his dam! Pete (Scammo), lives two properties down from me, and when he brought the land it had a house on it. One night we used the old house for a very big bonfire! We also play golf together. Greg moved into town from Darwin and brought the property just up the road from the pub. He plays golf too. Greg proofread my PhD for me before I submitted it and he did a great job. Greg collects all sorts of weird and wonderful things and his place looks like an antique yard.

Pup lives down the road from the pub. Pup does some work for me on the property with his tractor, which I call the orange peel. He dug out the area where the bio-diversity research pond is and I am thinking of getting him to do another one.

I used to drink at the local pub. This was where I would run ideas by people, see if I could get someone to help me do something. For example, at one stage I would make garden ornaments that I would sell at markets, and I stopped by the pub and got them all to listen to my ideas on where to sell it, and how much to sell it for, and if it would be something that would sell and make money. I stopped drinking there around 2013. I also used to play golf at the local golf club. I used to spend lots of time working on the course and having it ready to play on for visitors and locals. I stopped doing all of that following a few arguments with people and then I never played there again. This was also around 2013. At one point I stopped talking to most people in Bethanga. This was due to lots of things that happened around that time, but strangely I don't miss talking to, or interacting with any of them.

GIRRAGIRRA GANYA

girragirra ganya which means loosely, "happy place" or "merry dwelling," is the name I chose for the property at Bethanga.

I got the property listed as a wildlife sanctuary so the wildlife were protected.

It is surrounded by rolling hills and has a spring-fed creek running through it.

Mary-Anne and I used to get two fellas to come in and cut the grass and bale it up for us. When they finished, we would stack the bales on the ute and store them in the shed. We sold most of the bales when there was a bad drought on.

One of the many loads of hay.

When we first brought the property, it had around eight native trees on it. I eventually planted around another 5,000 trees. The planting made a huge difference to not only the way the property looked, but to the wildlife and birdlife that visited, making girragirra ganya their home. At different times there were goannas, echidnas, wombats, kangaroos and snakes living there. There were far too many bird species to count. Among my favourites were the magpies, which over time had come to trust me enough to let me near them. I was always visited by eagles. One day one of the eagles flew over my head, only missing me by about two feet!

The resident wombat at the time had a little echidna friend. The echidna, I noticed, would follow the wombat around everywhere. Nearly every night, or rather early in the morning around two o'clock, they would travel under the house to get to the pond for a drink. The wombat would lead, bumping into the steel posts on his way through. The echidna would follow along, scratching against the same steel posts and they would wake me up with all their bumbling about. After about an hour they would come back again, bumping into the posts on their way through. They were a funny pair, and I was relieved when I could finally get back to sleep! The wombat eventually got mange and went blind and died. His friend the echidna used to come onto the front deck of the house, lean up against the glass front doors and spend some time watching the TV! He was lonely, and I knew the feeling—but one day the visits stopped and I never saw him again.

The kangaroos were great. The joeys would play with the young cows and chase the young cows around in circles and then stop to have a break. Then the young cows would chase the joeys around in circles. Then the joeys and the adults would leave, but they always came back to visit, and then the romper room of fun would start again.

On most days, I would have someone come up and visit me. We would chat, have a few beers, sit around the fire in winter, or sit in the shade in summer. We would sometimes play darts or hit a few balls on the golf course we had built on six acres of the property. Pup was really great here, because without his expertise on the tractor, the greens would have been far too difficult to make. And of course there was the second pond that he made for me, too. It was good to do those things with friends and family.

As you can see, I had some great, great times at girragirra ganya, but twenty acres eventually became too much to look after on my own; not so much in a physical sense, but more in a financial sense. And so reluctantly I made the decision to sell. This was a very hard thing to do, but it was a decision that I made after many, many months of thought.

Besides, even though friends and family visited, I was still really very alone because there wasn't anyone to share the house with, share meals and stuff.

A beautiful but lonely lounge room.

Night times and mornings were the worst, except when Jacob had a sleepover. girragirra ganya, I had realised, was not a happy place or merry dwelling anymore.

girragirra ganya went to auction in May of 2018.

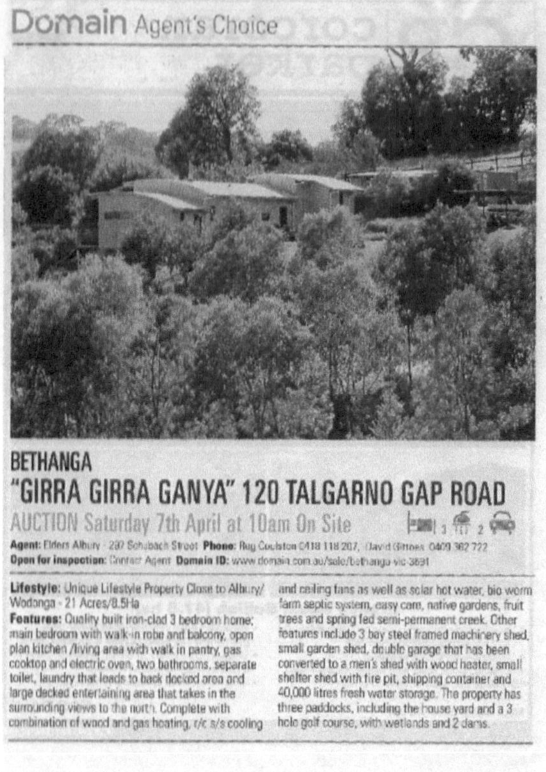

Girragirra ganya highlighting the new growth of trees.

A very nice lady and her boyfriend bought it and they moved there in June 2018. They are nice people and I was a little happier knowing that the property was in good hands. They have told me I can visit them and girragirra ganya anytime, but my visits are getting less and less, because there are just too many memories there, and I have to move on.

THE NEW HOUSE

After looking at and researching a lot of houses and real estate agents, I finally bought a house in a suburb of Albury, not far away from Daniel,

Sophie and the kids, and not far away from where Jacob lives. The house is a good house in that it is big enough for me, and has a nice split-level back yard. There is a lot of work to do to get it to where I will be comfortable, but this was what I wanted. I need to be busy.

I introduced myself to the people who live each side of me so that they knew who I was. One is a very, very nice lady. Her name is Ilona. Ilona and I speak often; mind you, I would like to chat with her more often. She invited me to have coffee with her a few times. There was one time that I drove her into the University so she could take some photos for me. Ilona paints and draws pictures of different things and she is very, very good at it to the extent that she sells some of her work.

My favourite painting by Ilona

Ilona is a real nice lady and she treats me with respect and always has a smile for me, and that makes me happy. We have coffee about every two weeks now, and we sit out the back on the patio, or in her backyard and talk. I cheat though! When it's my turn to buy the coffee, I get the large ones so it takes longer to drink and so in the end, we talk for ages! Hmm, maybe I shouldn't put that in? Not only is Ilona an absolutely brilliant artist, Ilona is great company and I hope our coffee moments keep going.

It's hard living in a new house. I have to get used to the differences in many things; the size of the house, the new noises and the new surroundings all have to be taken into account. That will happen eventually. And then when all the work has been completed, perhaps I will have a day when I will invite everyone to celebrate and we can share stories and things for a while once again. My Bethanga friends and Darryl do visit but only every now and then. I understand though, as it is hard to visit, have a few drinks and have a chat when they have to drive the twenty-five kilometres or so back to their own homes and families.

But to keep me in the loop, Jacob came shopping with me so I could buy a mobile phone. I hate mobile phones, but it's better than having to sign up to the NBN. I plugged the mobile in to charge it up and on the first day I melted the cover! I hate technology! My computer won't send or receive emails and so it is virtually useless and it looks like I will have to buy another one. I hate technology!

THE WAY IT IS

Darryl got very sick and has been diagnosed with cancer. He has under-gone chemotherapy a few times and it looks like it is doing him good. He is looking much better now and has just come back from visiting his brothers in Parkes, and doing some gold detecting with a mate. He likes living in Bethanga and I don't think he will move anywhere soon. The fella that owned the house where Darryl is staying sold it to a lady called Maggie. Maggie lets Darryl stay there and she looks out for him. I think that this lady is a truly wonderful person and I will always have huge respect for her. We all have our fingers crossed for Darryl. He brought a puppy dog back from gold detecting with him. He didn't have it for long though, as sadly someone drove over it and killed it.

Darryl had to go to Melbourne for an operation because they said he had a cracked bone in his back. But they didn't operate and then they sent him back to Albury hospital. A lot of the family came down to visit him in hospital and he was allowed to go home for a few hours as he was going stir crazy! Some of the family met with one of Darryl's doctors so he could tell us what was actually going on and what was going to happen in the future. We will know more when we have another meeting.

Darryl has been allowed home on a full-time basis. Lee, Gazza and Greg drop in to see him and he has others who help with housework and shopping and stuff, and I drive out and catch up with him as often as I can.

Darryl had to go back into hospital and whilst he was in there he decided that he didn't want to die in hospital. So he moved into his friend's house in Bethanga. He was only there for a short time though, and then he died. He is now in the spirit world with Mum and Dad. Darryl had asked that he be wrapped in paper bark before he was cremated. Jacob helped me get the bark and I took it into the funeral people and wrapped him in it. I have never been so sad in my life. I hope that I never see another human being look like Darryl looked that day.

To make things worse, when I went to pick up the urn, the funeral fella brought out a box and put it on the table in front of me and started to take something out. I asked him what he was doing and he said, "Oh that's right, you got the urn didn't you?" Then he got two pieces of paper and some sticky tape and started to make a funnel. I suddenly realised he was going to pour the ashes out into the urn right in front of me! I told him that there was no way he was going to do that while I was in the room, so he went outside and did it. When I picked up the urn with Dasher's ashes in it, I took it out to Bethanga where I could smoke them and so his friends could say goodbye to him. In a few weeks I will take the urn to Forbes where Darryl will be buried next to his Mother on April 5, 2019.

I drove up to Forbes two days before the ceremony and Jacob came up with me. Pete and Rob met us and we went through everything and how we thought things might work out. On the 4th we cut the branches and leaves and gathered some kindling for the smoking fire. Then early on the Friday morning we set everything up.

Setting up and getting ready for the smoking ceremony.

People started to turn up and we had a few drinks and waited for other people. In the end I think around 60 or 70 people came.

When it was time, I did the smoking for everyone and then it was time to say a few words and put the urn in the ground at Mum's feet.

I got a little emotional, and the words "he was a good bloke," seemed to be all I could say at the time. Then I covered the urn in ochre and put it in the ground. Everyone was invited to put some dirt in the hole and then we had some drinks and food and then people started to leave.

Then the hole was filled in and the urn was covered. When we had all packed up and cleaned up, Jacob and I left for home. By all accounts the ceremony for Darryl went really well. He is now with Mum and Dad in the spirit world where he is happy.

I am going along ok. I am still on my own and don't see this changing ever again, but it is something that I have to get used to. Worrying about it will not change anything. I used to get invitations to go to people's places for dinner, especially from Jackie, but I don't go because I don't have anyone to go with and I don't like going on my own. The invitations have stopped and that too, is understandable.

I'm still getting some work with the University and doing some Welcome to Country stuff.

Showing how it's done at a student smoking ceremony.

I get some work doing archaeological surveys, but this appears to have dried up lately. I have joined the Albury Golf Club and think I will soon get back into golf. I think both Lee and Scammo are going to join as well, which will be great. I sold my ute to my brother Pete for $500 and bought my first ever brand new car, a Honda Jazz; in hindsight I think I should have kept the ute for a little while longer. I still need stuff around the house and I have to get everything delivered, which means a delivery charge, which also simply means it costs more to get things done and the new car doesn't have a lot of room. The modern world keeps us all in chains, it seems. The more one has, the more complicated it gets.

The new car is scary to drive! It has two very, very bad 'blind' spots and sometimes, especially at roundabouts, I can't see cars coming. I can't see the bonnet and so it's hard to see if I am in the middle of my lane. I have to centre the speedo in the middle of the lane just so I know where I am! I have now traded in the Honda for an Isuzu ute. It is so much better having the ute and now I can start to get more done around the place instead of having to wait for someone to help me or having to pay big delivery charges…so much better!

I have decided to rent out two of the rooms in my house. I registered my house with the University as a place offering off campus accommodation. Around May a very nice girl came to have a look at the rooms and three days later she decided to take up the offer of a room. Her name is Aimee and I think that she is a very smart girl. Aimee is also a very beautiful girl, has a terrific personality and appears to be a very nice person. I think that Aimee could have been a world class model, she is that attractive, but she is going to be a dentist which is really good as she will make lots of people healthy and happy.

Aimee on her graduation day.

It's now June 7, and Aimee has moved some of her stuff in now and from the day that Aimee first had a look at the rooms until she moved in was around six weeks. The other room, hopefully, will be rented out by a girlfriend of Aimee's, which is really great. Now I have to fix some things up. This house is the coldest and hottest house I have ever lived in! I need to get a new air-conditioning system put in. The wood heater doesn't warm all of the house, and I need to make sure the girls are comfortable.

The other girl has visited and has decided to move into the other room. Her name is Amina and she, like Aimee, is a very nice lady. Amina is a Muslim girl and it will be very interesting having her here as a housemate. Well, Amina moved in, but then she moved out again! Seems that there were specific cultural rules that forbid her being here. That's a shame because Amina was fun.

Another girl, Kate, who is also a friend of Aimee's is now going to take Amina's room. Kate is also a very nice and respectful girl.

Kate and Aimee on graduation day.

Like Aimee, Kate cooks 'mysterious' food for dinner. I don't eat any of this stuff. Kate cooked up a cauliflower one night, but before putting it in the oven, she put some seasoning on it. It actually looked like a human brain! And it looked even worse when it was cooked! Yuk! But I enjoyed having Kate stay here even though she too was only here for a short time.

I was thinking about putting a swimming pool in the backyard but everyone tells me I'm mad! So I decided to put in an artificial grass putt-putt golf course instead. Trouble is, I know that the grass will shrink and this will cause problems, let alone the fact that it would cost around $1,000 to put it together. The jury is out on this one.

I don't get many visitors these days. In fact I have only had three visits from people since Darryl's ceremony. It isn't like it was when I lived in Bethanga. I get out to see friends, but most times they are either not at home or are doing work around their houses and I feel as though sometimes I'm interrupting. I think future visits to Bethanga may well be less and less, which would be a sad thing.

I'm getting a bit of work lately. I've done some surveys, some test-pit excavations and some Welcome to Country jobs, which is great, as the extra money will go towards the air-conditioning and painting the house. Hopefully more work comes my way. I was going into the University one day to do a Welcome to Country and as I was driving in I noticed some banners on each side of the driveway. On one of those banners was a photograph of me! If that wasn't scary enough, when I drove out of the place, there I was again on the other side of the banner. Yalmambirra looking at Yalmambirra was a very, very strange moment!

When I first bought the house I had taken into consideration that there was a fair bit of stuff that needed to be done in order to make it comfortable. In the twelve months that I have been living here I have spent around $19,000. But there is still more to do! Today the air-conditioning is finally going in. I can't wait until the house is warm and I don't have to wear a beanie inside to keep my head warm! And in the summer, I won't have to put a towel on the pillow to soak up the sweat because it's so hot! Gotta love air-conditioning. I have taken the wardrobe doors off and now I'm waiting to get sliding doors installed. The old doors were no good and the sliding ones I hope will make the room brighter and look bigger. Another friend of mine, Ben, has put new carpet throughout the house and has put new flooring in the kitchen and dining room. Great job, Ben!

Daniel has designed a football jumper for the local Rugby Union Club and it looks fantastic! I'm really glad he has done the design, and that it was accepted. I think that I may be invited to give the Welcome to Country at the launch of the design, which will be an added bonus and a terrific thrill for me. I'm very proud of Daniel.

Well, I did the Welcome to Country. I took Jacob with me because he was very proud of his brother. It started late and I didn't need to hang around so I told everyone that Jacob had a hot date as my way of getting out of there! He got the biggest cheers of everyone! It was really great to see Daniel's artwork on display and that there were around twenty-five football jumpers up for auction.

Steve and a mate came down to get Darryl's table that he had given to his daughter Lulu. The top of the table was supposed to be painted with Wiradjuri artwork. It got started and now Darryl's grandkids will finish it, which will be really great. My membership has run out for the Albury Golf Club. I'm not going to renew it because I don't want to play with anyone that I don't know and I really don't think that Lee or Scammo will ever join: they are still playing cricket! Scammo has leased

Jon and Joan's land and is currently running cattle on it, so I guess he has other things in his life more important than golf. Guess what? Ok I'll tell you…Lee has finally joined the Commercial Club! It was thanks to Jackie really, because she said to me that she would pay for the membership as a birthday present for Lee. Thank you Jackie!

I'm actually giving serious thought to moving again…yep! I've decided that once this place is where I want it to be, then if house prices are on the 'up' then I will sell and move to Parkes. At least I'll be able to get out with the brothers and do stuff, then instead of just sitting around and not doing much. Besides, if I was to get really ill, then it would be good to have the brothers around. The problem with moving is that I will be a long way away from Jacob and Daniel. Also I'm not sure how I will go in terms of getting some survey work, etc. The extra dollars always come in handy.

Steve, Pete and Rob came down for a game of golf the other day. There were the three brothers, me, Aimee, and Greg. Aimee was my partner and we ran last! The boys were only going to stay one day and night. After the golf they were supposed to put their stuff in the motel rooms and then get a taxi back to my place, have a few beers, get a taxi back to the motel, and leave the next morning. Well they didn't get the taxi and didn't get back to my place. Steve called me the next morning to tell me that they had decided to play another nine holes and then come to my place and stay the night and then go home the next morning! We ended up playing cards for about four or five hours. But through it all, it was good to catch up with them and they got on really well with Aimee, which was really great.

It's only about two weeks from going to Parkes for the 25th Anniversary golf weekend. This year we will remember Dasher, along with Dad.

Darryl teeing off on the 1st hole at Parkes golf course: for the last time.

The photo below shows family and friends in Parkes, to remember not only Dad and Mum, but Darryl as well.

It seems that there are going to be a lot of people there that weekend, but I think probably only around 12/14 golfers. I'm looking forward to catching up with everyone. Well, Parkes has come and gone for another year and it was a really great time.

Most of the family were there and a lot of friends. This year unfortunately, Lee and Greg couldn't make it, but I'm hoping that next year we could have it here in Albury…we'll see.

I've just finished doing a Welcome to Country for some NSW Water people. I asked a young Wiradjuri girl called Kat to give me a hand.

Kat and her Mum on Kat's graduation day.

We started collecting the leaves and kindling and then a lady came up to me and said that the first bus load of people would be turning up in around ten minutes. Ten minutes! It wasn't supposed to start until 5.30pm and here it was, just 3pm! Ten minutes later the lady told me that the next two buses would be arriving in fifteen minutes. Eventually we got through it all, and the lady came up to me and handed me a voucher as a thank you gift, which I gave to Kat for helping me.

A few days later Kat called me saying that she had to give the voucher back as it wasn't worth $25, but was worth $250! What an honest young lady…So I decided to take her shopping so she could share the voucher with me. Kat went back home to Wellington in Northern NSW to see her family at Christmas in 2019. Her Nan got really sick whilst she was there and had some really bad internal problems. Unfortunately, Kat's Nan passed away not long after. Kat is a very special lady and is terrific with technology stuff! It was Kat who gave of her time to put the photos in my story which helps to bring the story together. Kat's done a really great job because she also understood how important the whole thing is to me, and I am very, very happy with our selection and placement of the photos. I can't thank her enough.

I finally got the contact details for Kempy and Pinhead and sent them a message. Only Kempy has replied so far but it was great to catch up with him and talk about old times a little. I hope Pinhead calls me back as it would be great to chat with him. Maybe I have the wrong number? Well, I finally got to have a chat with Pin. He and Donna (his wife), have their own cleaning business, which is great for them. We chatted for a long time mostly about the 'good old days' but I told him that I would really try to get to his place for a visit. I'll call Kempy and see if he can meet me at Pinhead's and that way I'll be able to catch up with both of them at the same time…great stuff!

At this point in time (2020), there is a very bad virus that is affecting people all over the world. There have been a huge amount of people that have caught this virus and died as a result. There are lots of things that people are not allowed to do, and places where we shouldn't go. At the moment I really only go to the supermarket to get food, catch up with Kat when technology needs have to be met, and I still catch up with Ilona occasionally for a coffee, but that's about it. I, like everyone else, hope that the virus goes away soon…crossing my fingers!

It's May 14 2020. Two days ago Gazza called me up to tell me that my very good friend Pup, had passed away. This is really sad news and I know he will be missed so much by family of course, and by the many number of people who called him a friend.

THE END?

Well I think that it's time to put the jigsaw puzzle away for now. It isn't complete by any means, but as I had asked myself earlier: when is the jigsaw puzzle that is my life complete? I hope my story makes an interesting read for people who take the time. I'm not sure that I have made a significant difference in people's lives, but if I have then I hope that most of the differences have been good ones. Thank you to all those people that have called me friend throughout the years and that have stayed that way.

For much of my life I did not know I was Wiradjuri, and this discovery led to a desire to understand more about my cultural heritage and the land upon which I walk as I search for the pieces of my jigsaw puzzle.

I am Yalmambirra. It's who I am now, and it is who I will be for the rest of my life.

Attachments

The Attachments contain some of my thoughts on life, some of the works that I have had published and simply written, and some additional photos that people might like to look at. The newspaper articles about Lorna and Bertie are also included here.

BELOW ARE TWO OF MY THOUGHTS ON LIFE

YESTERDAY-TODAY-TOMORROW

Yesterday was tomorrow, the future
Then yesterday became the present
Yesterday then becomes the past…
Today was tomorrow, the future
Then today became the present
Today will then become yesterday,
the past…
Tomorrow is the future
but will become today, the present
Then tomorrow will become the past…

WISHES AND DREAMS

WISHES

Wishes are what we want
for ourselves, for others,
for things to happen,
or not happen…

DREAMS

Dreams my friends
are where our wishes
come true…

Yalmambirra 2019

PUBLICATIONS

Yalmambirra 2000, Black Time…White Time: My Time…Your Time. Journal of Occupational Science. Vol 7, No 3. pp. 133 – 137.

Yalmambirra 2004, Consultation and the Environment: Some Indigenous perspectives. Environmental Engineering Research Event. Environmental Change: Make it happen. Environmental Edge: 8th Annual Environmental Research Conference.

Zeldenryk, L & Yalmambirra 2004, A study of occupational deprivation: Australia's policy of assimilation. Australian Occupational Therapy Journal. Vol. 53, Issue, 1. 2006.

Yalmambirra, 2005, Qualitative research: a Wiradjuri perspective. Proceedings of the Second RIPPLE Qualitative Research as Interpretive Practice Conference. 2005.

Yalmambirra, 2005, Recreational Professionals: Knowledge and principles in relation to Indigenous peoples. Australasian Parks and Leisure Journal. Vol, 8. No. 1. 2005.

Yalmambirra & Spennemann, D H R 2006, Gawaimbanna – Gu Wiradjuri Nhurranbaang (Welcome to Wiradjuri Country). The 30th Annual ANZRSAI Conference for Regional Economic Development. Heritage and Regional Development. Regional. Association International. Australia & New Zealand Section Inc. 2006.

Yalmambirra 2006, Consultation as a Teaching Resource: A Wiradjuri perspective. Aboriginal Studies Association Journal. 2003.

Yalmambirra, 2006, Perceptions of Consultation: Indigenous Perspectives. Veg Futures: The conference in the field. Greening Australia. ACT, Australia.

Yalmambirra 2007, Knowledge and Wiradjuri: Who is telling the truth? A Wiradjuri Perspective. Sustaining Our Social and Natural Capital. Proceedings of the 12th ANZSYS Conference.

Yalmambirra 2007, Wiradjuri: Revival and survival. Northern Europe and its Indigenous minorities: Pointers for Australia? Centre for European Studies, UNSW, Sydney, NSW, Australia.

SUBMITTED

Yalmambirra, 2005, Wiradjuri: Pre-Invasion. Special Issue. (Indigenous Australia: Beyond the Margins / Beyond Marginality). Submitted to The Journal of Sociology for The Australian Sociological Association.

OTHER PAPERS

Honours Dissertation 2002, Heritage management in Wiradjuri country: Indigenous perceptions of consultation. Charles Sturt University. Faculty of Science and Agriculture. School of Environmental and Information Sciences.

Mungabareena Reserve – Wiradjuri Reconciliation Project-A 3 year journey: Community, consultation and contradictions. Presented at: The National Landcare Conference in Darwin 2003; the Indigenous Land Management Facilitators 6th Annual Workshop in Port Fairy (Vic) 2003; and in Geelong at the 5th Australian Network for Plant Conservation National Conference & Conservation Techniques Workshops 2003.

Consultation as a tool of Education 2004, Presented at the Indigenous Land Management Facilitators Workshop. Parkes, NSW.

Gawaimbanna – gu Wiradjuri nhurranbaang (Welcome to Wiradjuri Country) 2004. Presented at the Charles Sturt University Staff Colloquium in Wagga.

BEULAH ALBERT : SERN 3467 : POB FORBES NSW : POE MENANGLE NSW : NOK F BEULAH WALTER

I have looked into our native soldiers in some detail, but mostly dealing with our native LH soldiers. The problem recruiting natives was a problem in austrialia during the war as some states allowed there recruitment while others didn't. The problem also came into how native was each soldier, as some were not full caste but half caste or some caste then half caste. (how black is a a native soldier)? These are the known aboriginal LH soldiers I have on record;

BEULAH Albert 3467 Pte 01 LHR 30R tos Sig 7-18 (aboriginal)

near blindness'. By that stage, Abdullah was in his mid-60s, eking out an existence as a labourer. He would live just long enough to see citizenship rights extended to Aboriginal people.[65]

Colour mattered to the Department. That is nowhere more clearly seen than in the case of Trooper Albert Beulah. Having served in the 1st Light Horse Regiment, Beulah was a man of very 'dark' complexion. Inspector Doyle did not mince words about it. 'This case is not satisfactory', he wrote, 'the holder [of the lease outside of Forbes] is a black man'. Doyle noted Beulah 'had done nothing on his farm', neglected the fencing and seemed to prefer the easy money of driving a motor lorry. For 'altogether the wrong sort of man', forfeiture followed not long after. Again, the black man's own words tell a different story. Beulah's first dealings with the Department were a few months after taking up the holding. '[Will] the government pay the cost of putting in a well?' he asked. 'I have about one months' water in my tank, then I will have to stop ploughing ... you can see the position I am in. Hoping that you will look into this matter as it is urgent.' The Department's response was less than encouraging. 'Settler's application ... cannot be acceded to.' A report added that 'Beulah does not appear to know anything about farming'. Millennia of prior occupation counted little in the mindset of white administrators. When Beulah left the holding, it passed to HW Pearce, a man who 'would be an annoyance on any settlement'. Pearce's only recommendation seems to have been the colour of his skin.

> Mr Pearce is a stranger to the District and has made his debut by bringing
> a race horse (that is alleged to have won races before) as a Maiden ... [He]
> is a farmer but owns no land – possibly a Surry Hills farmer ... men that
> do this class of thing rouse a great deal of suspicion.

Between the lorry-driving blacks and shady characters like Pearce, the Inspectors at Forbes had their work cut out for them. Officials called again for a more restrictive definition of eligibility: 'Care should be taken that no other undesirable settlers be allowed' in the District. And in that there was an irony. Men like Beulah belonged to the country in a way whites never could; they had created the landscape carved up, quantified, commodified and degraded by soldier settlement.[66]

These three files are all the more remarkable because they lend voice to Aboriginal soldier settlers. Despite being marginalised by white society, Indigenous veterans claimed their rights and entitlements under the soldier settlement scheme, asserting their equality with every other returned digger. A powerful sense of moral economy informed that discourse. It is the subject of Chapter 3.

Previous System Number	Loan Number	Surname	First-name	Land District
[12/7220]	7134	BEULAH	Albert	Forbes

(1928-2012) Music – opera singer

A Wiradjuri woman from Forbes, Lorna Beulah learned the piano and began singing from the age of 12 years. After formal singing lessons and marriage, she sang at night clubs, parties and weddings, before moving to Alice Springs where she won the National Aborigines' Observance Day Committee's talent quest in 1962. This provided a scholarship to the NSW State Conservatorium. Following her first radio appearance with the ABC in Sydney, Lorna sang to crowds in Martin Place where she received a standing ovation and was named 'The Nightingale.' She appeared in the Australian premiere season of *Porgy and Bess* in 1965 and performed on television with *Bobby Limb's The Sound of Music*, and Graham Kennedy's *In Melbourne Tonight*. Lorna sang with Jimmy Little and Harold Blair; appeared in many operas, including *Oliver*; and was invited to sing at the Sydney Opera House before it was opened to test the acoustics

Lorna Beulah singing in Martin Place on National Aborigines Day, 1964.

AND THE SUCCESS OF TWO

Two Aboriginal artists have made great strides since they were given an initial helping hand some years ago by the National Aborigines' Day Observance Committee. 'They are mezzo-soprano, Lorna Beulah, formerly of Alice Springs, and well-known entertainer, Col Hardy, who originally came from Brewarrina. Miss Beulah, whose married name is Mrs. Oliphant, and who lives at Toongabbie, near Sydney, won the 1963 N.A.D.O.C. talent quest. She and Col Hardy sent recording tapes to Sydney.

Their artistry was immediately recognised by N.A.D.O.C. officials who brought them to Sydney and set them on their way to their present success. Miss Beulah is studying at the Sydney Conservatorium

by courtesy of Sir Bernard Heinze. She has passed her audition for the Australian Broadcasting Commission, and will give a concert over the A.B.C. radio at 9.45 p.m. on the evening of July 9,

National Aborigines' Day. Miss Beulah has already appeared on Bobby Limb's highly rated T.V. musical show, "Sound of Music."

STAR-STUDDED SHOW

FOR NATIONAL

ABORIGINES' DAY

Jimmy Little, shown here signing autographs for two of his fans, will compere a unique show which will star leading Aborigine performers on the eve of National Aborigines' Day—July 12. The revue will be staged in the Anzac Auditorium, College Street, Sydney (opposite Hyde Park) on the night of July 10 and will be repeated the following night. The artists who will head the bill are Lorna Beulah, who recently made her classical debut, concert singer Harold Blair, and pop singers Betty Fisher, Noel Stanley, Jimmy and Fred Little, Col Hardy and Candy Williams.

National Aborigines' Day highlights will be the usual rally in Martin Place on Friday, July 12 between 12.30 and 1.30 p.m. The Governor, Sir Eric Woodward, the Minister for Education, Mr. E. Wetherell, and Sydney's Lord Mayor, Ald. H. F. Jensen, will be the principal speakers. Others who will address the rally will include Harold Blair, Mr. James Warburton of the University of Armidale, Mrs. McAllam, of the Sydney Nurses Association, and Mr. J. Brown, of Worragee.

The weekend celebrations will end with a rally at the Central Methodist Mission on Sunday, July 14.

DAWN, *July*, 1963

Jimmy Little, shown here signing autographs for two of his fans, will compere a unique show which will star leading Aborigine performers on the eve of National Aborigines' Day—July 12. The revue will be staged in the Anzac Auditorium, College Street, Sydney (opposite Hyde Park) on the night of July 10 and will be repeated the following night. The artists who will head the bill are Lorna Beulah, who recently made her classical debut, concert singer Harold Blair, and pop singers Betty Fisher, Noel Stanley, Jimmy and Fred Little, Col Hardy and Candy Williams.

National Aborigines' Day highlights will be the usual rally in Martin Place on Friday, July 12 between 12.30 and 1.30 p.m. The Governor, Sir Eric Woodward, the Minister for Education, Mr. E. Wetherell, and Sydney's Lord Mayor, Ald. H. F. Jensen, will be the principal speakers. Others who will address the rally will include Harold Blair, Mr. James Warburton of the University of Armidale, Mrs. McAllam, of the Sydney Nurses Association, and Mr. J. Brown, of Worragee.

The weekend celebrations will end with a rally at the Central Methodist Mission on Sunday, July 14.

DAWN, July, 1963

Above: Daniel, Pete, Darryl and Jeremy.

Below: Me, Daniel, Pete, Darryl and Jeremy.

Me, teeing off with Greg watching.

Rob, Steve, Me and Pete.

Greg watching where his ball went.

Below: Me, Rob, Darryl, Pete and Steve.

Mum having fun with Jacob.

Jacob in the snow…tastes good!

Jacob with his mate Migay.

Jon, me and Shaun.

Kempy.

Pinhead.

My first plane trip.

Rochelle and Shaun.

The sign on the box reads "Quiet please, exam in progress."

Paddy melon bowls to pass the time away on one of the desert trips.

A rest well deserved out in the desert.

Desert trip girls bringing wood for the fire.

They haven't seen the snake yet! A desert trip surprise.

A desert trip break.

SCORECARD

Names			H'cap		Scr	Nett
Player/s:						
Marker:						
Hole	Player/s	Marker	Hole	Player/s		Marker
1	4		10	4		
2	3		11	4		
3	4		12	3		
4	4		13	4		
5	4		14	4		
6	4		15	4		
7	4		16	4		
8	3		17	3		
9	3		18	3		
Par	33		Par	33		
Score			Score			
			Total			

girragirra ganya scorecard.

Some photos of Darryl's funeral.

Mum and Darryl.

Darryl, Mum, Me and Terry.

THE TWO FACES OF KAT

THE POEM

AS IF BY MAGIC

How lovely she is, this child of mine
Like a flower opening for the very first time

AS IF BY MAGIC…

Watching her play, Mother Earth and me
With the other kids, what a joy to see

AS IF BY MAGIC…

They came out of the bush
The whitest I've seen
Emptiness now, where she'd once been

AS IF BY MAGIC…

They never brought her home
That child of mine
Like a flower opening for the very first time

AS IF BY MAGIC…

The hurt and the pain I feel everyday
The tears in my eyes they won't go away

AS IF BY MAGIC…

Reconciliation…again

AS IF BY MAGIC…